I'M COMING APART, LORD!

DOES THAT MEAN I'M A DISCIPLE?

I'M COMING APART, LORD!

DOES THAT MEAN I'M A DISCIPLE?

LaJoyce Martin

I'm Coming Apart, Lord!
Does That Mean I'm A Disciple?

Copyright © 1997
LaJoyce Martin

ALL RIGHTS RESERVED
No portion of this publication may be reproduced, stored in an electronic system, or transmitted in any form or by any means, electronic, mechanical, photocopy, recording, or otherwise, without written permission from the author. Brief quotations may be used in literary reviews.

FOR INFORMATION:
LaJoyce Martin
202 South First Street
Morris, Oklahoma 74445

ISBN: 1-57502-685-6

Printed in the USA by

3212 East Highway 30 • Kearney, NE 68847 • 1-800-650-7888

Other Books by LaJoyce Martin

The Bent-Winged Series:
To Love a Bent-Winged Angel
Love's Mended Wings
Love's Golden Wings
When Love Filled the Gap
To Love a Runaway
A Single Worry
Two Scars Against One
The Fiddler's Song
The Artist's Quest

Pioneer Romance:
The Wooden Heart
Heart-Shaped Pieces
Light in the Evening Time

Historical Romance:
So Swift the Storm
So Long the Night
To Strike a Match
Destiny's Winding Road

Historical Novel:
Thread's End

Western:
The Other Side of Jordan
To Even the Score

Path of Promise:
The Broken Bow
Ordered Steps

Children's Short Stories:
Batteries For My Flashlight

Nonfiction:
Mother Eve's Garden Club
Heroes, Sheroes...and a few Zeroes

TABLE OF CONTENTS

Introduction	9
A Traveling Disciple	11
A Willing Disciple	17
A Singing Disciple	23
A Working Disciple	29
A Remembering Disciple	33
A Scared Disciple	39
A Renewed Disciple	47
A Determined Disciple	53
A Worried Disciple	61
A Dining Disciple	63
A Rejected Disciple	67
A Sentimental Disciple	73
A Thinking Disciple	77
A Doting Disciple	83
A Happy Disciple	89
A Protected Disciple	97
A Faithful Disciple	101
A Weary Disciple	107
A Runaway Disciple	113
A Hurting Disciple	117
A Blessed Disciple	123
A Mellowing Disciple	127
A Growing Disciple	135

Introduction

They'd been traveling in pairs without a credit card.
They'd been shaking off the dust from their sandals.
They'd been shucking devils.
They'd just interred murdered John.
In the hustle and bustle of life, they hadn't the leisure to eat, much less rest. They were disciples.
Then the Lord told them to "come apart."
This book is dedicated to those who sometimes have that "coming apart" feeling. I'm a disciple in your boat.
We're rowing hard.
We know that it's difficult to get across the Red Sea when we're seeing red.
We often fear that our Sea of Tiberias is spelled "T'-bury-us."
Our resources have gone overboard in the storm–the rigging, the tackling, the cargo. We hope we're not next.
We've had it from A to Z. Accused. Bruised. Criticized. Downtrodden. Effaced. Faulted. Goaded. Hassled. Indicted. Jabbed. Knocked. Lambasted. Maligned. Negated. Opposed. Plundered. Quashed. Rejected. Scorned. Torn. Undermined. Vexed. Worried. X-rated. Yoked. And Zapped.
But we're still rowing. And we remember that when the

I'm Coming Apart, Lord!

disciples of Jesus "came apart" in the book of Mark, He was with them.

That's the beauty of discipleship. In our storm-whipped little ship, we have His fellowship. His friendship. His leadership. His guardianship.

Okay, we're coming apart, Lord. Doesn't that mean we're disciples?

A Traveling Disciple

"Why not write a book about all those wild experiences on the road?"

"No way."

"Aw, c'mon. Why not?"

"Because nobody would believe the stories, and I'd be mad when the book landed on the fiction shelf."

You see, I've read too many Zzzz-rated autobios. The kind that put you to sleep. I don't like solemn, sedated, statisticial scenarios. I'd just as soon skip the dreaded baby book with its inky footprints, tooth slobbering testimonials and misquoted monosyllables.

Who cares that I weighed eight pounds, I was born on April 24 when Herbert Hoover was President, and it took my dad a year to pay Dr. Pyke the delivery fee? (Stork postage was cheaper back in Nineteen Hundred and smurfsmurf.) Who cares that I got a rubber duck and an orange for my first Christmas and that I was in love with Little Boy Blue embroidered on my baby quilt? That's boring.

I would rather go directly to the nine priceless–that means

I'm Coming Apart, Lord!

we didn't get paid, doesn't it?–years with a traveling preacher, an experience synonymous to a trip with the prophet Jonah to Tarshish. Threaded somewhere among that half million miles, I learned that a traveling disciple must have three unalienable G-forces: grit, gumption and God. Greenback would help, but it's alien.

Did I keep a diary throughout that near decade (to be interpreted "near decayed") of trying trekking? Heaven forbid! I was too busy keeping the Sabbath at twenty-four days an hour to manage a log. Besides, writing while riding put seasickness to shame.

So I just thought and rode, rode and thought. Some of the thoughts even nauseated me.

Looking in the rearview mirror, I realize I should have written a whole book gleaned from a lifespan of episodes packed into one nine-year eternity. Please forgive me, but I couldn't. Extenuating circumstances held me hostage. On my husband's pittance, I couldn't afford pencil and paper.

We started at a bad time, back in the sixties when costs were going up so fast a dime wasn't worth a nickel; in a bad way, we had just been abruptly dismissed from the church we pastored; and under bad circumstances, with a very active one-year-old son. By age two, our child was even more active, and by three, he was totally hyper. A previously owned marimba red Pontiac, a single piece of obese luggage and our youngster summed up our life's possessions. To those who understood my tongue in cheek humor, I sent a picture of our toddler emerging from a suitcase with a caption beneath: "Shut up, and get back in that suitcase!"

The fourth member of our team was Smoky Bear. He was stuffed and short napped and had shiny eyes, which also describes the little boy who drug him from pillow to pillow. We had bought him with green stamps. I've forgotten how many books it took or

A Traveling Disciple

how many years it took us to collect them. The service stations that green stamped were always more expensive on their fuel, and my husband shunned them like a leper colony.

Smoky Bear attended all functions and with a bit of help became quite lively when the music began. Church was dull neither for him nor for those sitting nearby. But, lo! One catastrophic night he was left sitting on a pew in Oklahoma. That meant a hundred mile trip that night to retrieve him. Because of his distinquished bravery in that dark, unpeopled building, he won a seat in our attic's Box of Fame.

After three harried years of sleeping in church annexes, basements, cockroach incubators and not so spare bedrooms, we found a bedraggled, much used Yellowstone travel trailer. Oh, joy! It had no air conditioner, a bathroom the size of a footlocker and green shag carpet that had long since shagged out.

Ah, at last. A place of my own! I embraced it as my preinherited mansion from Heaven. However, after a few weeks of living in the seventeen foot crate (that measurement included tongue and tail), I changed my mind about the heavenly bit. Especially when someone donated my son an Easter chicken, and he caged it in the shower. On a scale of one to ten, the fowl smell rated a thirteen.

"You should be pleased," my husband sallied. "I've provided you a home with a 7'x15' living room, a 7'x15' dining room, a 7'x15' kitchen, a 7'x15' office, and a 7'x15' bathroom!" Note that there was no mention of a bedroom in my "home, home with the mange" because there was none.

Had I contemplated a book back then, it wouldn't have been *Please Don't Eat My Plastic Plants* or *Please Don't Cry In The Instant Potatoes*. It would have been *Please Don't Sit On The Baby*, for in the four years that we were blessed to possess this

I'm Coming Apart, Lord!

abominable abode, two baby girls were spawned, joining our nomadic lives. We added a 7'x15' nursery.

The original child took his insecurity blanket and moved under the table. Betimes, the one spindly leg of that collapsible shelf gave way, and the apparatus along with its contents spilled onto the head of the poor dear beneath. (He still blames me for brain damage.)

Now there were ten in the trailer: two humans, three humanettes and five angels. If angels can be nominated for admission to neurological wards, I submit our five as deserving candidates. They earned their nervous breakdowns.

I've tried to put myself in their wingtip shoes in hopes of understanding their chagrin when they learned they were assigned to us. Can you imagine their reactions when they first saw that ugly "homeaside"? Eggshaped. Oxidized. Blessed with patches where fins of the fifties had gouged its loins. Baking in the West Texas sun. I can just hear them.

"You mean we all have to live in that? All ten of us?"

"How will we keep our robes without spot or wrinkle?"

"Why, the sink isn't as big as my halo."

"And no air conditioning yet. Will they expect us to fan them?"

"The humans will sleep on the couch, but where will that humanette sleep?"

"The specs say there will be *three* humanettes."

"Three?"

"Yes. The diagram shows one sleeping under the table."

"And I suppose we'll have to stay up all night and hold the others?"

"I'm worried about getting my wings squashed."

"Or singed."

A Traveling Disciple

"Or sat on."

"We might co-author a book on 88 ways to fold your wings and—"

"A good idea. And make enough money to buy a bigger trailer."

"I'm turning in my resignation. Today."

"Don't kid yourself. The time sheet says we have seven years of this before any of us can retire."

"Seven years of that sickly green carpet? Why, it could harbor garter snakes, bubblegum, thumbtacks or—"

"Oh, quit griping, all of you. God doesn't sponsor sissies. Now everybody count to ten. Ready . . . Set . . . GO!"

Poor angels.

A Willing Disciple

"Can we keep him, Mom?"

The small dog stood beside my eight-year-old son, his ears perked to attention. His alert, searching eyes traveled from Kevin to me and back again as if the question belonged to him, too. Scarcely out of the pup stage, he was a bit undernourished but very clean. His radar detector had zeroed in on the transmitter of Kevin's heart, and he'd followed the beam to our temporary home.

It was love at first sight for both of them. Kevin had begged for an animal, dreaming of fun-filled days with his own dog at his heels. And here was his answer.

"Can we keep him, Mom, huh?"

An ache filled my heart, a familiar pain that I had lived with for six years. Our migratory lifestyle denied our children the pleasures of anything permanent.

"Son, you know we'll be leaving in two or three weeks," I explained weakly. "There would be no way to take the dog with us."

Kevin said nothing. He just turned and walked away, his head down.

It wasn't the first peeve I'd had about pets. In Alabama I

I'm Coming Apart, Lord!

had persuaded Kevin to give up the chicken who lived in our 2'x2' shower stall. He could have a beautiful goldfish, I promised.

But even that turned out disastrous. I sat the quart-sized fishbowl in the sink for the trip to Tennessee so Goldie wouldn't "spill." When we stopped for the night, the poor dear was still in place, trying to peer through the bubbles. A bar of soap had slid into his (or her) watery world. He/she didn't survive.

Was it my imagination, or were the tests getting harder to pass?

Later in the day, Kevin returned with the dog. "Mom, I'm naming my dog Pretzels. Is that okay for a name?"

For all the world, the scrawny little thing looked like a pretzel, his honey colored hair dotted with white frosting here and there. I laughed in spite of myself.

Ignoring my mindset, Pretzels became an integral part of us all, showing his gratitude in numerous small ways. He was noiseless and polite. Had he been in pooch politics running for "World's Greatest Dog," I would have voted his ticket simply because he never once turned over my trash can.

"Don't you think he's gaining some weight, Mom?" Kevin asked after a week of smuggling goodies to his friend. He stroked Pretzel's head fondly.

"Sure," I agreed then hurried back to my work to drown out unpredictable emotions. *What will happen when the revival ends and we have to leave the dog behind?* The nagging dread camped in my subconscious without a flashlight.

"Pretzels and I are going hunting," Kevin would inform cheerfully each afternoon. Then taking his BB gun, he and Pretzels would head for the fence row just beyond the trailer, oblivious to the future.

Why must life's good days pass so fast and the miserable

A Willing Disciple

ones so slowly? This was a special time, a special place. If I could just call Joshua to stop the clock! The pastor, a millionaire, had insisted that we leave our tiny trailer behind and allow him to accommodate us in a large mobile home that he owned. Any time away from our shrinkwrapped existence seemed like a furlough from the Battle of the Bulge for all of us.

Reshaped, our trailer would have fit into the kitchen of this gigantic home on wheels. There were two whole bedrooms in his mansion versus none in ours. And there was actually room around the dining table for regular sized chairs! Our baby celebrated her first birthday in grand style with her own borrowed high chair.

Kevin's whole personality took on a change. He had a special tenderness in his voice as he talked to his younger sisters, the same tone he used with Pretzels. He was kinder, more loving in word and deed.

"Pretzels is doing marvels for Kevin," my husband remarked to me one day. "He isn't the same child."

"But what will happen when we have to leave Pretzels behind?" There! I had verbalized my fears. But my husband could not answer that haunting question.

"There's no way, just *no way* we could take a dog." He shook his head sadly.

I knew that was true. We barely had enough room for three children. We wouldn't be doing the animal justice to squeeze him between the guitar and the port-a-crib.

Each evening Pretzels followed us a full block to the corner to see us off to church. And when we returned "home" again, he was patiently waiting beneath the trailer near the steps as our welcoming committee. And such tail wagging!

Travel, insecurity, leaving behind a toy bicycle were all Kevin had ever known. We had started our tour of duty when he

I'm Coming Apart, Lord!

was a mere fifteen months old. Two weeks here, three weeks there or six weeks in yet another location was our mode of life. Arizona, Colorado, Kansas, Oklahoma, Georgia, Alabama, New Mexico, Arkansas, Texas, . . . Were we being fair to our children? The two girls were not old enough to be affected by the constant uprooting, but what was all this doing to Kevin, who was at such an impressionable age? How could I bear to kneel beside his bed in the months to come and hear him sob for Pretzels?

Each time I broached the subject of parting with the dog, Kevin chose to ignore the subject. He'd whistle for Pretzels, and they would sprint off on another venture.

I don't know how intelligent dogs are, but I feared that Pretzels sensed the approaching day of abandonment. We got a merciful reprieve when the revival services extended a week beyond normal. Yet I couldn't decide if this was a boon or a barb since each day welded Kevin's devotion more solidly to his friend. It might be less painful in the long run to leave and get it over with.

Pretzels trudged moodily close at Kevin's side the day we started loading the car for departure. His eyes became two giant puzzles as clothing, suitcases and instruments were piled into the back of the overburdened station wagon.

"If there was any way we could take the dog, . . ." my husband said in hushed undertones. We knew it was hopeless. A neighbor down the road promised to see that Pretzels had a good home.

Pretzels raced us to the corner as usual; then he stopped. My husband drove slowly. Kevin had stationed himself in the back of the wagon among the piled to the roof luggage. He pressed his nose against the rear window and watched the dog as far as he could see.

A choking lump came to my throat, and it took an amend-

A Willing Disciple

ment to my constitution to hold back the tears. Glancing sideways, I saw that my better half was fighting an identical battle. But we couldn't cry; we had to be brave! What could I say if Kevin burst into a frenzy of tears? I feared I'd rupture, too. A mother's inner tube can only stand so many pounds of pressure.

As the last glimpse of Pretzels faded, I heard my son say softly, "Goodbye, Pretzels. . . ."

And with that, Pretzels was gone from our lives forever.

In the months that followed, Pretzels' name was never mentioned. It was as if he had never existed.

Months later, Kevin was asked to write a composition about a dog for his "school at large" literary assignment. I waited anxiously to see what he would write. Sometimes, I had learned, he put into story form feelings that otherwise went unexpressed. Would I at last learn of the remorse in his heart over the loss of his "very own" dog? Would he write of his beloved Pretzels?

He didn't. Instead he wrote about a generic brown dog named Cocoa that he had played with briefly at a young cousin's house.

It was then I began to realize the quality that my child had developed over our years of travel. He had an ability that not even I as an adult had mastered–to leave the yesterdays behind and to accept the dreams of tomorrow.

How fortunate he will be, I thought, as he gleans from each transient friendship its best then goes on to other great adventures! In learning to leave behind life's joys, he will likewise be able to leave behind the sorrows. Maybe he isn't such an unfortunate child after all.

In the ensuing months, this disciple found herself praying, "Dear Lord, grant that I, too, can as willingly and completely give up the things of life that mean so much to me–the friendships, the

I'm Coming Apart, Lord!

small material possessions, the joys of yesterday–and go forward to a new day without looking back in remorse to blessings left behind."
  Goodbye, Pretzels.

A Singing Disciple

In a moment of intense insanity, I wrote a four-wheel limerick with a piracy of the "Home, Home on the Range" tune. I tried to bait the lines of the song to synchronize with:

> Home, home on four wheels
> Out on God's harvest white fields
> Where seldom is seen
> Any money that's green
> And you have to trust God for your meals.

It wasn't quite appropriate for church services, and Nashville didn't want it. It was neither religious nor secular. Actually, I found it quite impractical for anywhere.

I decided a prayer would probably do me more good and would go straight to the point. No need to play games.

"Now, God," I'm afraid my voice was a fret high, going right to the top like a flag going up a pole, "what is to become of me, dragging three little children all over creation, going farther in the hole each day?"

My body shaped itself into a horseshoe around the altar of

I'm Coming Apart, Lord!

a small clapboard church in central Oklahoma. Nobody was in the building but I. Nobody visible, that is. I needed answers and on the double. My nerves didn't have much tread left.

We had crawled into town with a badly bleeding transmission, polluting Highway 35 with a stream of motor oil. The old Pontiac's odometer showed 200,000 miles, and the travel trailer we pulled behind us would have won the ugly abode contest.

We had traded the seventeen foot Yellowstone for a twenty-one foot off brand that had been in a hurricane in Galveston, salvaged by an insurance company. Nobody wanted it but us, and we just thought we wanted it. Small wonder it wasn't in demand. It was a freak of the trailer species, the only one like it anyone had ever seen. A mutant. Built like a box within a box, it expanded and contracted hydraulically. Watchers would stand and gape as it lost inches but not weight.

That is, if it was in a mood to close up at all. Once open to its full width, it often balked at going skinny again. Then we had real troubles and resorted to coaxing it shut with hammers, jacks, pipes and other such lethal weapons.

I hated the carpet in that trailer. It was a yucky yellow, its shaggy strands long enough to French braid. But the bathroom was a full foot broader than the one in the single-wide, and all of us could sit around the kidney-shaped table if we didn't mind stacking our feet in a neat pile underneath.

The two baby girls were still in diapers, the proof reeking from a plastic diaper pail in the closet. Having the bucket made a lot of scents. On our income, we couldn't afford full-time Pampers; that luxury was reserved for babysitters or conventions.

Costly array wasn't one of our venial sins, either. I made the children's clothing on a portable sewing machine donated to me by a matron of mercy. I used double knit scraps garnered from

A Singing Disciple

strangers, designing my own patterns. The garments were hot items only because the material was so thick. I never mastered the zipper fly in my son's pants, so he wore them elastic waisted with a seam in the front until he was half grown.

Both my husband and I lived with a pre-ulcer horror that we would have a medical emergency with no insurance to cover it. (A Mutual State of Anxiety.) With three children, we figured a crisis wouldn't be hard to accomplish.

"Lord, we have no CDs, no money in the bank, and we don't even own a credit card! Judging from the itinerary of small churches we have on schedule, we'll do good to get from one location to the next. Motor oil could consume our fortune. The future doesn't look very bright for us—"

I don't know how God speaks to other people, but as I sobbed silently–and then not so silently–a beautiful song flowed through my spirit until it seemed my soul would explode with the melody of it. The tune, one I had never heard, came along as a bonus. I realized that the song, born not of talent or trend, was an inspiration from God in response to my "what is to become of me" question.

Hurriedly, I unhorseshoed myself from the altar, went to the piano and began to sing with my untrained alto voice:

> I.
> Jesus carefully weighs each trial
> Knowing how much I can bear;
> Promising faithfully all of the while
> I'll never have more than my share.

I'm Coming Apart, Lord!

Chorus:
All my tomorrows must pass by the Lord
Before they come to me;
All my tomorrows must pass by the Lord
From here to eternity.

II.
Sorrows must pass God's measuring rule
As well as each heartache and tear;
This is my weapon against Satan's tool
Of uncertain tomorrows I fear.

III.
Sickness and death must pass His test
Before they are placed upon me;
In His sweet promise my heart can rest
"I won't put too much upon thee."

A recitation also came with it:

My tomorrow came before the Lord.
"And what do you hold in your span?" the Master asked.
"A trial," my tomorrow said.
"A trial? Then wait!" said the Master. "I must measure it and see that it isn't too long. I must weigh it to make sure it isn't too heavy. For, you see, I have promised my children that I would never put more

A Singing Disciple

upon them than they are able to bear. And have you any joy to take along?"

My tomorrow just hung its head.

"Then you cannot go until you can take along enough joy to make life worth living. And what about grace? Here! Take some of My own grace, for I've promised grace sufficient to meet the needs of the pilgrim journey all the way from earth to glory."

And so if Jesus delays His coming and my tomorrow arrives, I need not worry. I need not fear. Because all my tomorrows must pass by the Lord before they come to me.

The four-wheel song didn't matter anymore. Wings had borne a weary disciple to higher thoughts, to another song. This one was copyrighted in Heaven.

A Working Disciple

Small churches were our specialty. "They need us," we told ourselves to boost our egos. We did try a big church once, hoping the dough would rise. This is where the Jonah analogy comes in; we belly-flopped. I mentioned the lack of audience response to the pastor's wife. "Oh, our church is used to the *best!*" she said. Obviously, we weren't.

I must admit, I didn't make the best grades on the meek disciple test, either. "Any church that can't respond to plain ole preaching out of the Bible is sick," I retorted tactlessly. We never got asked back.

We specialized in small offerings, too. At one place, we conducted a Vacation Bible School (sans supplies to spare the sanctuary's savings), a children's choir to allure adults to attend, a daily radio broadcast, baptismals in the city park, plus nightly revival services. All for $25 apiece each week. Although the collection was much more than that, the parson chose to keep the rest for himself.

Our lodging was provided: in a boarded-up cubicle in the trunk of the church that was the worse fire trap I had ever seen. I awoke at every smell. Those two weeks cost me seventy times

I'm Coming Apart, Lord!

seven.

I might have become rich and famous had I written an exegetical exposition on the Biblical phrase "instant in season, out of season." It would doubtless have been a blockbuster. We had a penchant for doing things out of season. Blotting up Arizona's 130 degree ground temperature in July. Scheduling Louisiana for the flood and fever prime time. Blowing into Kansas with dancing tornadoes and jackknifing on Colorado's black ice during the dead of winter. Each incident had its own tale to wag. Our itinerary never seemed to correspond with the elements or vice versa.

Then our firstling turned six, and our school at home hit a snag. My opponent's name was Philip, a perma-set agnostic. He didn't like our war against his drugs, his overt role in the city's abortions or his alliance with Satanism. He threatened to turn me in to the authorities for teaching my child without a state license. "Oh, please, don't do that," I begged with mock alarm. "When the school officials come to the trailer and see what a good education my child is getting, they will want to send me ten more young'uns to teach, and I just don't have time to teach more kids!" He never mentioned it again, but he did offer us a thousand dollars to get out of "his" town. We stayed and had a great revival.

I practiced minimizing the minuses and maximizing the pluses, pretending they weren't really minipluses and maximinuses. After all, who else got an unpaid vacation twenty times a year? Who visited more state parks, drank more clear water, had "holier" socks or got to spend more time with their parents than we?

Traveling disciples risk coming apart every few days. My wool-gathering cannot imagine Heaven without a celestial KOA, a little roped-off section where all traveling disciples camp in golden Airstreams complete with diamond hubcaps. On the banks of the crystal river, beside the tree of life . . .

A Working Disciple

You might even find a damp rope hanging on the tongue of an aureate mobile or a lounge chair under the gilded awning. Yes, and you might find someone like me who yearned to write on earth with a coveted sapphire pencil.

My nine years of traveling have now melded into ancient history. I live in a home with three emergency rooms and an office for my very own electric pencil sharpener. No more bathing kids in a mixing bowl, using the tablecloth for a crib sheet or storing Tide in the oven. But, alas! Now there are jingling telephones, hospital visits, choir practices and midnight counseling sessions. And those endless salad suppers . . .!

I'm settled at last. Hooray, I'm on the road to writeousness! I'm ready to sprout pen feathers. Let's see, I was going to entitle that book "Please–Don't—"

I grab my 200-sheet spiral notebook and reach for my #2 yellow pencil. Hey! What is that fork doing behind my ear?

A Remembering Disciple

"Mom, I want to make a cake."

Angella, the older of the two younger children, held a box mix in her hands. It was chocolate. Did you ever know a child whose first cake wasn't chocolate? It has something to do with the color in direct contrast to the white formica on the countertop.

"Mom, I want to make a cake" are words which strike terror in any mother's heart. Especially if the child is making a maiden voyage on the journey of cookery.

"Let me turn the oven on for you."

"Oh, *Mother!* I'm no baby. I can do that."

"It might explode."

"Your cakes never explode." With cake on the brain, she bypassed the oven.

That was an imaginary conversation, but it well could have happened at my trailer/house/apartment/basement.

I've never understood why it should take seven bowls (assorted sizes) and nine spoons to mix any battered substance. Or why every first time baker with her apron sagging to her knees has to lift the mixer out of the bowl while it's running. Or lick the spoon between every stir.

I'm Coming Apart, Lord!

If I had a syndicated advice column, I'd say the best thing for any mother to do is get out of the kitchen. Pronto. With my daughter's announcement, I did the best thing for all concerned. I disappeared.

In reading the directions on the back of the box, Angella thought 3/4 cup of water meant three or four cups. She dumped in three full cups and a little extra for good measure.

Then she turned the oven to 350 degrees and waited for the pastry to cook.

And waited.

And waited.

And waited some more. Two hours passed, and it still didn't look right. But good news! By the third hour, it was becoming chewier. We spooned it out and tried to eat it, for all good parents eat what their children cook. We would have done better with straws. I was proud of her; she invented the first drinkable cake. I thought she ought to get a patent on it and insure against product liability–if prosecuted, plead the Fifth.

We never finished that cake. Two members of the family claimed to be allergic to chocolate. I took one look at the kitchen and was never quite sure what made me ill.

I could have laughed at Angella for her mistake, but I dared not because I remembered. . . .

I remembered twenty-five years aforesaid. My first pie.

In my pre-wed era, I had not cooked. My mom, healthy, hearty and a handsome cook, handled her kitchen singlehandedly. She needed no help and never mentioned wanting any. My growing years were swallowed in a whirlpool of attending school, working an eight hour a day job, dating and frequenting church activities. Learning to cook wasn't on my list of priorities. Indeed, it wasn't on my list at all.

A Remembering Disciple

I misfigured that knowing how to cook came along with marriage like the cord to the coffeepot. As with motherhood, I reasoned that the knack would be there to meet you when you arrived. It would come naturally.

Not so. I was fortunate that my groom had batched for two years and knew how to make gravy, else we might have starved. It took me a long time to get the hang of making gravy. Its consistency seesawed from watered down soup to Crisco. And I never did master the biscuits.

But back to the pie. The oven was just large enough to accommodate a ten inch pan. I had in mind some palate pleasing, double-crusted fruit concoction. I could just taste it! I knew better than to try one of those fancy meringue things that could get weepy between layers or cry amber teardrops on top. I didn't want to try anything that could double-cross me.

To this day, I don't know how I managed the crust. Someone had given me a recipe book as a wedding gift, but most of the cooking language was foreign to me. Words like braise and baste and blanch befuddled me, and I hadn't the funds to hire an international interpreter. A few recipes did have step by step pictures, though, and that may have included crust. I could cope with pictures.

How does a fruit pie get thick? I wondered. I puzzled and pondered but came up with no answers. Finally, I broke down and called an elderly lady across town to ask if she could tell me how to thicken a fruit pie.

"Why, certainly," she offered. "Use cornstarch."

Simple enough. However, my knowledge of starch only included one kind: Faultless laundry starch. But then, if it made clothes "stiff," why not my pie filling? Why hadn't I thought of that myself?

I'm Coming Apart, Lord!

"I only have the blue kind," I mentioned, mentally locating the starch in the cabinet beneath the sink by the drainpipe. "Will the color make any difference?"

When she regained her voice from the laughter unsuccessfully suppressed, my dear old friend educated me just in the nick of time. Otherwise, my husband might have walked stiff-legged forever.

Then there was the time I tried to make tapioca pudding, the Jello brand in the little square box. I had never heard of tapioca, but it sounded good, kind of tropical. The problem was that I didn't know that it was supposed to have those bumps. When they would not cook out, I threw the whole recipe in the trash. I didn't want my new husband to see the mess I'd made of the lumpy pudding.

My own mother could have laughed at me when I told her my story, but she remembered. . . .

She remembered another twenty-five years earlier. Back to her first dessert for her brown-eyed sweetheart. It was a chocolate pie. She baked it with love, topped it with a mound of whipped cream, then slid it into her ancient galvanized oven for the cream to brown. Unfortunately, it puddled instead.

All of us have made mistakes so that none of us may point an accusing finger at another of us who fumbles the ball. A couple of thousand years ago, some people wanted to throw rocks at a neighbor who had fallen. Jesus in His defense of the woman (St. John, chapter eight, verse seven) suggested that the first stone be cast by one who had never done any wrong himself. That limited the number of throwers to zero.

Nobody had a perfect record. As each man remembered, as his conscience convicted him of his own unlovely past, he dropped his rock and walked away, forgetting the charge he had brought against the neighbor. Nobody was "worthy" to cast a stone except

A Remembering Disciple

Jesus. And He chose not to.

In rearing my children, I often reminded myself that verbal rocks can hurt as badly as flint and granite and shale. I spilled cereal, tore my best dress and cried over silly things when I was a child, too.

Even today when I am tempted to criticize, ridicule or slander, I remember. . . .

And when I remember, I choose to forget the wrong done by another.

Let me be a remembering disciple, Lord.

A Scared Disciple

I'd never flown anywhere (except off the handle) before I met Elroy Martin. When I married him, I had no idea that he was fly infected. I tried to swat the idea away, but it didn't do any good.

I would find AOPA (Aircraft Owners and Pilots Association) magazines in strange places, and we couldn't pass a Mobil service station without his longing gaze pivoting to the flying red horse. I soon learned that all the water in the Tasman Sea couldn't quench his love for aviation.

In spite of my hysteria, my pleading, begging and screaming, when we had been married five years, he went to ground school and passed his written test to be a pilot. However, it took the next seven years to wedge in his minimum forty hours air time for the flying exam. (A small matter of funds was involved.)

"Airplanes are safer than cars," Hubby contended. "I have statistical proof." Proof or no proof, I was unconvinced. With every airplane story he told, my fears multiplied like guppies in a fish tank. Take, for instance, the two brothers in Arkansas who attended our revival. They taught themselves to fly with no instructions whatsoever. They wore out two sets of tires racing up and down

I'm Coming Apart, Lord!

the runway, getting the "feel of it." Then they managed to clear the end of the tarmac and land abruptly in a pasture, sending cows with packed bags packing in every direction. The amateur pilots were none the worse for it, but when I heard the account, I was.

While revivaling in Albuquerque, my fly-bitten man ran across a childhood friend who had acquired flight instructor status. The generous buddy offered his services at no charge. "I'll solo you," he promised. So my mate made his first sky trip alone. No one cut the tail off his shirt–the traditional initiation for first time soloists–but he was so happy he could have popped the buttons. I was petrified!

Shortly thereafter, another streak of bad luck took us to a series of services near the Colorado border where yet another sympathetic friend offered his plane. "Take it to finish out your hours," he said.

With two and two-thirds children, I spent my daze alone, a plane widow, in our spacious seventeen-foot trailer that was frozen to the ground. My calendar said June, but actually it was December. While my husband frolicked in the air with the angels, I was down below dealing with mortals and earthly woes, which included the proprieter of the trailer park. "Don't put apple peelings in the commode," he accosted me with a frosty frown. He didn't mention potato peelings. Was one biodegradable and the other not?

Then the car took cold and wouldn't start. It coughed and sneezed. Then it died. We walked several blocks to church on solid ice. I hoped I didn't slip and lose the whole maternity I'd been working on for six and one-half months.

We sat through the Christmas holidays, cold and lonely, with icicles for decorations. If we just had transportation! Necessity is the mother of invention, but I became the mother of necessity. I left the hair dryer running under the hood of the car all night. The car

A Scared Disciple

started the next day.

When my avid aviator lacked only nineteen minutes of his precious forty hours, he racked up that remainder on the way to Durango to meet the FAA examiner for the flight test. He passed with flying colors on a field of white snow. We were both ecstatic, but our static was on different frequencies. I was thrilled to have him on the ground again.

The chance to use his flying skills for a worthy cause came unexpectedly a year later. While conducting services in Amarillo for Cousin Royce, that relative got a call to speak at a funeral miles removed. Feeling too ill to drive, he prevailed upon my husband to fly him to his destination. His wife, Annette, needed to go along to sing for the rites, and she wanted me to keep her company. She had arranged for sitters for her two children and my three.

At 6 p.m. on January 26, Elroy began checking with the weather bureau. The report was marginal, and he worried the telephone until midnight before weariness won.

"If the report isn't better by daylight, we don't fly," he said. I hoped the skies would be closed to all traffic except to a few soaring prayers.

But, no, a cloudless day greeted us the following morning! The tower assured us that no change in weather was due for several hours. Getting five small children prepped for the caregiver, servicing the rented aircraft and studying aeronautical maps didn't give me the time I needed to work up a proper case of nerves.

"God, keep us in the cocoon of Your protection," Cousin Royce prayed as the four of us bowed our heads. That was his standard traveling prayer. I hoped to stay a moth in that cocoon instead of awakening as a butterfly in another world. I figured my prayer rated the most urgent on God's chart of fervency anyhow.

Cessna 172, with her 5631 Alpha call letters, lifted us from

I'm Coming Apart, Lord!

Tradewinds Airport and bore us into the smogless horizon of the Texas plains. The knots in my stomach loosened. But near Abilene, a few scattered clouds necessitated a drop in altitude. Even harmless clouds gave me palpitations.

"We'll stop here, eat and check the weather reports," my husband informed us. While we ate our hurried lunch, he refueled and checked forecasts covering the surrounding areas.

A cold front was moving in, he was told, but we were safe for at least five hours. We would be at our designated port in less than two. The clouds had lifted, and again the sun gave us a two-faced smile. However, a sixth sense was at work on our pilot. "Perhaps you should go from here by rental car," he suggested to Cousin Royce.

"Oh, I couldn't possibly make it by car now," Cousin Royce objected. "We're too far away. I'd miss the funeral! Besides, the weather looks fine to me." And indeed, it did.

"Then let's hurry!" My husband herded us toward the craft, and with only a short delay by the wake of a jet, we set sail again.

It was my first cross-country flight, and I was just beginning to relax and enjoy the patchwork below. Reading the chart, Cousin Royce informed us that we were right on course and making excellent time. *See, this isn't so bad after all,* I said to me.

Then, without warning, we hit the subtle weather front head-on and three hours ahead of time. With each minute, visibility dropped. Moisture began to form on the windshield; the temperature took a frightening plunge. Looking behind us, we realized that we were socked in from every direction.

"We're only six minutes from a small airport," our pilot said, "but I'm going to land. I think we could make it, but I can't chance icing. We're going to land now . . . on that road down there." He circled twice to determine landing feasibility on the farm-to-market

A Scared Disciple

blacktop then swooped for the emergency landing.

"Watch your airspeed! Watch your airspeed! Watch your airspeed!" Cousin Royce sounded like a phonograph with its needle stuck and the volume turned too high.

Like Peter in jail on the eve of his execution or Daniel in the den, Annette had gone to sleep. She suddenly awoke. "Is this the airport?" she yawned.

"No!" I barked. "We're going to crash land!"

"Well, where's the airport?"

She was so calm I wanted to shake some terror into her. I felt panic to the tenth power, and here she was nonchalant. Unabashed. Not even *scared*.

"Pray!" I begged her. "I have babies to raise!" Nobody else could put up with my three children, not even an orphanage.

Our circuit took us over two highline wires and under the next. "Lower. *Lower!*" Cousin Royce turned up the pitch. Our pilot fought a tough crosswind, manuevered past trees and a bridge and brought the aircraft to a superbly smooth stop on the hilly two-lane highway.

"Wow! That was fun!" Annette squealed. "Let's do it again!"

If looks could kill, she would be going to another funeral–her own.

Annette and I occupied the back seat, and neither of us wore a size four. When the two men climbed out of the cockpit, our weight caused a shift in the balance polarity. The nose rose and the tail fell, sending the airplane sledding backward. I yelped with fear. Annette laughed.

The men arighted it, pulled it off the road and tied it to a fencepost. A slightly inebriated farmer offered to drive us into town where Cousin Royce arranged for the continuation of his trip,

I'm Coming Apart, Lord!

leaving us behind.

My eyes met my husbands', our spiritual telepathy working well. "We aren't here by accident," I said. We had gone down a mere fifteen miles from Grandmother's old homeplace.

"No," he agreed. "We aren't. God has a plan for us."

Grandmother had left us the year before. The last time I saw her, she was propped in an ancient wooden rocker, still mumbling incoherent prayers. She must have caused the vials of heaven to overflow with the tears she spent for Frances, her backslidden daughter. Yet when death ended her forty years of filling vials, the wayward one was still wayward. Now Grandmother was gone, so why were we here?

For four days we were grounded under the ice storm that wreaked havoc over the entire state. It was Sunday before a clear day allowed my husband to return the rented plane to Amarillo.

I didn't make the return trip with him; the nightmare of our narrow escape was too fresh in my memory. I wouldn't give those almost motherless children another opportunity to be orphaned.

Instead, I made my way to a small, old-fashioned church to worship. Its wooden benches and open-faced heaters reminded me of Grandmother. She loved this church. It was her church, where she attended her last service on earth.

There couldn't have been more than a dozen people there that evening. The pastor was away on a trip, and the local farmer left in charge asked if I would say something of inspiration to the small group who had braved the weather to attend the meeting. I'd done little public speaking and certainly wasn't a minister, but I was willing to give my ten percent if God would finance the other ninety.

I stood behind the old Bible stand, bowed my head and sent up a desperate SOS. What could I say? How could I be a blessing? When I looked up, Frances, the wayward one for whom Grand-

A Scared Disciple

mother had wept and prayed, walked in.

I cannot think it was anything these paltry lips uttered that touched a chord in Frances' heart that night. But as the tears coursed down the lines of her repentant face and she found her way back to God, I knew that the Lord had discovered some vials on the prayer shelf of Heaven labeled "The Wayward One."

God's plan for a plane has never been plainer than the plan for 5631 Alpha.

The man I love has been a pilot for more than a quarter of a century now. The daughter that was my two-thirds child when he bagged his bird license is a pilot, too. The fears that once plagued me seem foolish as we skirr about the skies on speaking sprees.

Why the change? I know more about airplanes, their ways, their natures. I know about radios and the navigational systems. I know about runways and towers and beacons. But better than those, I know my pilot. He will do everything possible to see that I have a safe journey. Say, he handled a crisis grandly, didn't he?

Oh, yes, I've been a scared disciple. I've feared crashing, drowning, burning and death. I've had the jitters about clouds and mountains and power failures. But I'm learning to trust my Pilot. He's brought me through a few emergency landings lately. . . .

A Renewed Disciple

I hate back braces, but during a bout with my back, I gave up and wore one. The velcro outfit squeezed me at the waist and almost cut off my breathing. I tried to be as optimistic as I could.

"Look!" I told my husband. "Now I have a thirty-two inch waistline."

He glanced up from his flying magazine. "With gusts up to forty," he countered.

He was right. My bulges were simply rearranged, pushed to other portions of my body above and below.

My mind somersaulted back to a time when instead of taking my problems to God and "shedding" them, I had tried to push them into another room and close the door.

We tried a short (and ineffective) pastorate sandwiched between our first year and last eight of traveling. Why that church voted for us will leave me forever wondering. After we arrived there, they didn't want us, and we in our glorified ignorance were too daft to realize it. We thought everybody loved us. Ouch!

We lived in the back of their church building in some converted Sunday school rooms. Our furniture, picked up at

I'm Coming Apart, Lord!

auctions, garage sales and thrift stores, called for dark sunglasses. The refrigerator was pea green to mismatch the blue-green curtains. The ancient Duncan Phyfe sofa glared out over a modern hardrock maple coffee table. A black naugahyde recliner with a vibrator skulked in the corner.

Nothing correlated with anything else, people or furniture.

Determined to make good, we mowed lawns, drove hundreds of miles for hospital visits and fed the poor. We would win through warmth, love and self-sacrifice. The church began to grow, and so did I. We discovered that our first child was on the way. We were elated.

But the element of dissatisfaction among the saints never slept. We'd made no Brownie points with them. We were too young. Too inexperienced. Too much like a previous pastor. They complained about the way my husband held his handkerchief. He had a habit of folding the sneezecloth into a square that wasn't kosher. I doubt if God Himself could have pleased them.

We rode that bucking bronco for two years. Then we lost the stirrups. They called a meeting and demanded our resignation. Out we went. Within twenty-four hours, we had taken our pea green refrigerator, the baby and his bed, our wood veneer stereo– and fled.

I clung to the scripture, "When He hath tried me, I shall come forth as gold," but I didn't even feel gilded around the edges. I was tarnished!

We were welcomed to return to the road with plenty of engagements and invitations. But I couldn't forget the injustices done to me. Here I was trying to do my best and was rewarded with the worst! It was something of a disgrace to be impeached in those days.

I became aloof. People had hurt me, and I would see that

A Renewed Disciple

my heart stayed behind its bulletproof vest from now on. They'd not get the chance to injure me again. On this foundation of distrust, I laid a frame of self-pity. I crawled into my shell to lick my wounds. Life's service road had too many potholes, and I didn't care to travel it anymore.

I cinched up my emotions, sending my resentment to less girded spots for the duration of each revival. Then I'd meet them head-on. With gusts up to forty.

We hadn't purchased a trailer yet, which was probably a blessing. I may have used a secluded place of my own as an incubator for more bitterness.

Ten months after our abrupt dismissal, a beautiful thing happened. A church in Oklahoma scheduled us for an indefinite amount of time. I dreaded it. I didn't know the pastor or his wife. I wasn't in a frame of mind to make new friends . . . or enemies. And horror of horrors, they insisted that we stay in their home! They had five small children, and we had one. That was ten people under one roof. What kind of crazies would volunteer for such chaos?

I soon learned. When I tried to shut that wonderful, patient pastor's wife out of my world, she and love had a wit to win. Alma prayed with me, for me and about me every day. We had been there a week before I realized something was healing on the inside.

One October day I awoke anticipating morning as methodic as the grocery list: put on easy care polyester clothes, return nighties to suitcase, make up bed, lay out play suit for baby, . . . This morning seemed a carbon copy of all the previous ones.

Leaving my yearling asleep in his bed, I slipped into the kitchen to find Alma dressed in street clothes. "I may have to leave any minute," she apologized. "I got a call to be on hand for a home delivery."

I'm Coming Apart, Lord!

"A human?" I blurted. I thought home deliveries went out with the spinning wheel. I didn't know the stork still went from door to door like the Schwan man.

She laughed. This lady had come dangerously close to breaking my protective armor in the short time I'd known her. "It's all new to me," she said. "Barbara doesn't even attend our church, but she wants me to be with her. She lives several miles out. This will be her ninth child."

Alma wasn't much older than I. Did I see apprehension and uncertainty flit across her face? Perhaps I did, but I saw something else, too. I saw compassion that reached past her own church door, past her fears. The only prerequisite was a need.

Something nudged me, some bulge I'd tried to rearrange. I was habited to detaching myself from a demand of any kind or transferring it to my overburdened husband.

"Would you like to go along?" she asked.

"I'll go." It was more than a decision; it was a sudden compulsion. "At least I can sit in the car and pray." Drafting our husbands as babysitters, we left about noon. A bumpy lane took us to a frail trailer. The family's home had been destroyed by fire, Alma said, and they would soon rebuild. Three vehicles sat in the yard: one belonged to the family, one to a friend and the third to the midwife.

Alma disappeared into the mobile home. The car became my prayer chapel, observation tower and solitary confinement. My eyes followed as a three year old followed his father, who followed a mower that ate Johnson grass behind the lodging. Nothing outside gave any indication of what was transpiring inside. Time dragged.

An hour later, Alma summoned me. "Why don't you come in and sit in the living room?"

So I began the second stage of my vigil in the minuscule

A Renewed Disciple

living room/dining room/kitchen that scarcely cleared my head. Exactly what I expected I don't know. Whatever it was didn't happen. My ear, tuned to hear moans, metered only silence and calm, low voices.

Alma came again. "She is in a great deal of pain and asked if you would join us in prayer." I stood outside the bedroom door and bowed my head.

I do not know what propelled me to my knees beside the bed of a woman I had never seen. But as I grasped her hand, a smile crept across her face. She was a pretty woman, mid-thirtyish, dark eyed and dark haired. She seemed woefully tiny in comparison to my own large frame. I gladly would have taken her place at this moment, and I knew she felt that.

The harder she gripped my hand, the more fervently I prayed. Yet as her labor landed its last blows, she did not cry out. The pressure on my hand told its own story.

I prayed more fervently. Her struggle became mine. *Covering twenty-one states in ten months, we've encountered crises of every shape,* I thought. *Except this.*

Then a nine pound, one ounce boy tumbled into the world, protesting. He was cyanotic. "Blue babies, good heart," the midwife said, sensing my concern. "Ashy-white ones, bad heart."

When the baby gave his first lusty, spontaneous cry, I realized I was crying, too.

I followed the midwife into the living room. "A rough delivery," she said.

"You delivered the others?" I asked.

"No. Only the last three. Barbara has a history of difficult deliveries. The first and second were C-sections. The doctor advised against more. The third and fourth were instrument births. With the fifth, she begged the doctor to allow natural childbirth. He

51

I'm Coming Apart, Lord!

said he would if she wouldn't holler and scare his other patients. She checked into the hospital then checked out again and went to her church for the courage she needed. When she checked back in, she had confidence that she and God would make it fine. Her baby was born in thirty minutes.

"I've been with her for the last three, and none of them have been easy. But this is the way Barbara wants it."

The family friend dressed the baby and brushed his shiny black hair. I held out my arms for him.

My heart was pounding, my mind racing. He's breathing. He thinks he's hungry. He needs a diaper changed already. His nails need clipping. The miracle of birth!

Had there been only one birth that day, fate would have failed in her supreme purpose. The second took place in my heart. When I took a stranger's hand, I "shed" my own bitterness, and a new courage was born. Courage to live again, give again.

I was a renewed disciple–with no more gusts up to forty.

A Determined Disciple

Everyone needs an accomplice to accomplish anything. This chapter is really about my brother, Bobby. There were only two of us to wreak havoc on our parents. He was three years my junior and endowed with all the good looks. He was often mistaken for Elvis Presley. We never had much sibling rivalry, but there was plenty of sibling revelry.

Take, for instance, the time I slipped into the back floorboard of an old couple's car–a widow and widower–on their date. (They're long gone, and there's no chance for an exposé, thank heavens.) They were parishioners in Dad's church, and Dad knew nothing of my wickedness that night. My faithful brother followed at a safe distance to rescue me from any harm that might befall me.

When the chivalrous gentleman walked his lady to the door of her house, I snuck out of the car and was picked up by Bobby. I had a sweet story to tell everyone except my dad.

In the spring of 1968, Bobby lived in Louisiana, and I didn't live anywhere in particular. The advent of my second child was lurking dangerously near, and we had moved our speaking engagements close to the hospital. Mom and Dad had an RV pad in their orchard, a lovely nest, only seven miles from a brand new clinic

I'm Coming Apart, Lord!

where my daughter would join us.

We were ministering twenty-five miles north and east, and a strange lot that congregation was! Their attention span was below C level. A whimpering child, a door opening or outside noises set them to looking around instead of listening. They were worse than a primary Sunday School class when the wind is blowing.

We divined that if I played the piano very softly throughout the whole service, we could lasso their wandering attention and keep their thoughts corraled. The music drowned the devious distractions.

On the night of May 12, I played until after 10 o'clock, and my back hated me for it. The next day, Angella was born.

I had only been home from the hospital for a short time when my brother called. His wife hadn't been feeling well, and she thought a trip would help her. But before he got to us, he called again. She was feeling worse, and he couldn't care for their eighteen-month-old baby and continue to drive, too. (That was before the day of car seats.) Mom and Dad went to meet him.

When they all arrived, Pat wanted to hold my new baby, but her arms would hardly support the seven pound weight. It worried us. She said she didn't hurt anywhere, though, and she had no fever. She thought she'd be fine in a few days and insisted that we not call a doctor.

Then quite unexpectedly, she lapsed into a coma. We called the ambulance; she died two days after she was admitted to the hospital, never regaining consciousness. The same hospital that brought our bundle of joy now saddled us with overwhelming sorrow. An autopsy showed a heart defect that none of us knew she had. It had not appeared on any previous medical examinations.

Bobby was devastated. It hurt me to see his hurting. I had seen him hurt before. When he was six and I was nine, he fell out

A Determined Disciple

of the car traveling seventy miles an hour. Thinking he was rolling down the window to toss an apple core, he pulled the Chrysler's door handle. The wind jerked him out. I thought the car had run over him. My voice left me, and I couldn't tell Mom and Dad what had happened. Bobby survived, but it left a scar on my mind.

That was bad, but this time he was hurting worse. His world was dark. Pat was the light of his life, he said, and the light had gone out suddenly. She was twenty-six.

He moved back to Mom's and Dad's home with his baby girl, Kimberly. In the months that followed, he kept a diary to record his anguished thoughts and feelings. On one occasion, he wrote that he felt directed to West Texas and a town named Dumas. He had recurrent thoughts of an orphaned girl.

The thoughts disturbed him greatly. He asked himself, "Will Kimberly be an orphan? Will she be deprived of both parents? What does it all mean?"

The year after Bobby lost Pat, our car broke down in Dumas, and he came to help fix it. He was there over a weekend, and we all attended church together.

The young lady directing the children's program that Sunday morning wore a simple black dress and had her hair "stacked on top," giving her a look of maturity well beyond her years. She was still in high school.

"Who was the young lady in charge of the children's program this morning?" Bobby asked that afternoon.

"Oh, she is an orphan that a family in the church took in," I said. "Her name is JoAnne."

West Texas? Dumas? Orphaned girl? The diary . . . ? Into the wee hours of the morning he wrestled with unanswered questions. Finally, he cried into his pillow, "Oh, Lord, if this is Your will, You work it out!" He dropped into a restful sleep.

I'm Coming Apart, Lord!

The "God, if it is Your will" entailed a whole week of overhauling the car's motor (three times) only to find nothing amiss the last time it was torn apart. Why wouldn't it run so Bobby could be on his way?

An Australian missionary came to speak on Friday evening. He felt so sorry for us and our lame car that he prayed for the motor that night. He asked the entire church to join him. The next day it started.

JoAnne was in charge of the refreshments after the missionary service. Bobby developed an unquenchable thirst for sodas and bought the entire platter of peanut butter cookies she had made. He returned home with her picture in his billfold.

"Mommy!" Kimberly cried with joy when she saw the picture. She begged to see it often, to hold it in her hands. When Bobby wrote a letter to JoAnne, Kimberly scribbled love notes on the bottom, chattering, "Writin' to Mommy. I wuv Mommy!"

When the couple announced their engagement, JoAnne's friends asked what household items she would need. "I don't know what Bobby already has," she said. "I'll write and ask."

"You mean you would use his first wife's things?" someone questioned.

JoAnne was shocked. "Why not?"

"Well, I wouldn't!"

JoAnne's answer showed her mettle. "Must we throw away nice things because she used them? Must we discard Bobby's shirts because she ironed them? Shall I not touch the baby she held? No, I refuse to be that small."

She'll do, I decided.

She could hardly wait to get back from her honeymoon to her little girl. "She will never feel like a stepchild," she vowed. And indeed, she didn't. Although JoAnne later bore three more children,

A Determined Disciple

none was dearer to her than Kimberly.

When Kimberly was old enough to understand, JoAnne invited me to go with her and the child to the cemetery where Pat was buried. She had bought a rose for Kimberly to put on the grave. "You had another mother, but God took her to Heaven," JoAnne explained as the child placed the flower on the headstone. It was a beautiful experience, full of wisdom and devoid of trauma.

JoAnne loved and stood by my misfortune plagued brother. They had been married five years when a propane tank exploded as he welded nearby, sending him and the vehicle being repaired spiraling from the carport into the yard. The west end of the house was hashed.

Jars of home-canned relish, stored in the carport, burst and sprayed their contents on Bobby's head. He pulled himself from the rubble, freeing his broken arm, and surveyed himself in the car's mirror. Thinking the mess in his hair was his brains falling out, he went into shock. I got on a cross-country bus and went to Arkansas to assure him that he would survive this, too. When I arrived, I hardly recognized him, but with time and care, he returned to his handsome self.

Years later, with four children to feed and to care for, he went to work for Trotter Ford as a painter. He walked around the police car he had masked off. It would be ready for its initial coat of paint first thing Monday morning. The windows were covered and the chrome protected with tape.

It's almost time to go home, he thought, *and I'm glad. It's been a long week.* He opened the back door of the car and looked in. Police cars fascinated him. With the grate between the front seat and the back, it would be impossible for a criminal to harm the driver. Or would it?

The rear doors had no inside handles. Once a lawbreaker

I'm Coming Apart, Lord!

was in, he couldn't get out. But if his arm was small enough and he could slide it up beside the front seat, . . . ? Would that be possible?

Bob climbed into the back seat, careful to leave one leg out to prop the door ajar. He pushed his arm between the frame and the seat. He could almost reach around it. Maybe if he changed positions, . . . The area in the back was quite cramped; could one even get both legs in?

Concentrating on his efforts, he twisted around, pulled his foot inside and closed the door by habit. Too late, he discovered he was trapped inside the car.

At first he thought rationally. *There will be a way to get out.* He tried to break a window. No luck. He tried kicking and pushing and pounding. No luck. He used his pocketknife to dig and gouge and turn everything. No luck.

Then he had an idea. He would release the front seat lock, and it would fall forward and hit the horn. With the incessant honking, someone would come on the run! The idea died a horrible death. He remembered he had disconnected the battery.

Now he began to panic. It was Friday afternoon, almost quitting time. If he didn't attract someone's attention, he would be here until Monday, a gruesome thought. Would there be enough oxygen inside the interior of the cab to sustain him? It was miserably hot! Would he die of heat exhaustion? Or thirst? Or hunger?

His wife wouldn't know what had become of him. She would be frantic. His four children would cry when he didn't come home. And nobody at all would think to look here.

One by one, doors closed and employees left. Would anyone come back to the paint shop?

He heard footsteps. Through one tiny crack in the paper that robed the windows, he saw a man. He shouted, but the man

A Determined Disciple

couldn't hear him. He had to stop that man! With his pocketknife, he pecked on the window as loudly as he could.

The man stopped. He had heard! Looking toward the roof of the tin building, the man considered. "Hmm," he said. "A bird. A woodpecker." He walked on briskly.

Bobby's heart fell. That was probably his last chance to be rescued from his weekend prison. He fought spasm after spasm of fear.

The big shop door closed with finality. Footsteps again. The man was coming back through on his way out for the day.

Bobby pecked then let up. He pecked some more, a pattern of heavy staccato beats. *Oh, God, let him hear me.*

The man paused again. "That woodpecker sure is a determined bird," he muttered and started away. He scratched his head. "But why would he be pecking on a metal building?"

Something made him turn back toward the car. He realized then that the pecking was coming from within the vehicle. He opened the door and let the scared "prisoner" out.

Bobby made it because he kept pecking. But that wasn't anything new for him.

Determined disciples may feel backcombed and teased until they're sure that if life ever gets untangled, a great hunk of it will be left in the brush.

Determined disciples may be shipwrecked, beaten, stoned and left for dead. But they never give up. Huh, Apostle Paul?

Determined disciples keep pecking.

A Worried Disciple

Uncle Willy was a silver-haired man who lived by the Golden Rule. He rarely spoke, but when he did, every word weighed a hundred pounds.

For the sum of his ninety years, Uncle Willy lived in the bottom lands of Oklahoma on a small acreage staked by his grandfather when America was newborn. It was a haven for us city-weary and soul-battered nieces and nephews.

There was a hammock in the trees, a cold water windmill, a fishing pond and a half-broken filly. Uncle Willy milked his own cows, churned his own butter, and his industrious wife made jellies and jams from the native fruits to complement her homemade breads. Guests were a joy to them, and we dropped by as often as our busy schedule allowed. Our hectic life was a world removed from the quietness of the farm.

On one particular visit, turmoil dug trenches in my mind. With five hungry mouths to feed, a ghastly electric bill and a Mercury that smoked and drank, the struggle to make ends meet had become a frightening challenge. One misstep and we would be off the cliff and ruined financially.

Gangrene had set in on my faith, and I was fuming about

I'm Coming Apart, Lord!

inflation. Prices were going up while our income wasn't. The buck didn't stop anywhere! How could we survive? Where could we cut back? I worried that our outgo might outstrip our income, causing our upshot to be our downfall.

Uncle Willy patiently let me have my say; that was his way. Then he spoke seven words, slowly and with that hundred-pound-each punch. "I've never known inflation to bother God."

I was young. Uncle Willy was old. He had seen droughts and storms, crops and failures, good years and lean. He had learned that when God said He'd supply for the needs of His children, He took inflation into consideration. I said no more. I'd had my lesson for the day with all its assignments.

Many years later, it seemed we were again boxed in, doomed. High medical bills, a car accident and illness stripped us of our resources. What now? Should we file Chapter 11 for reorganization? Chapter 13 for extended payment? Or would we be pushed to Chapter 7 . . . bankruptcy?

If I could call Uncle Willy back, what would he say?

Suddenly, I knew!

He'd let me stew for a while. Then he would hand me his thrifty seven words. I can almost hear him now. "I would suggest you try Chapter 23."

"Chapter 23?"

"Of the Psalms."

Good advice for a worried disciple.

A Dining Disciple

When I was in school, my classmates gave a comical recitation of a teenager's stomach. The stomach did the talking, and although the details have escaped me, the gist of it went something like this:

"Ho-hum. Here it is 7 a.m. and time to try to get going. I surely hope this is a better day than yesterday. Yesterday was terrible! It's 7:30 now. Oh, no! Here comes a dill pickle! I wasn't quite ready for that. And . . . Coke? At this time of day? Ugh. Whoa! I'm not in the mood for that chocolate candy bar I see sliding this direction. . . ." etc., etc.

On and on the stomach went through the day, bemoaning the poor eating habits of its proprietor.

I'm afraid our stomachs did a lot of talking during our nine years in Roam. Who could blame them? If we are what we eat, that's scary. Nutritionists claim that diseases, lack of energy, poor general health and even untimely deaths are credited to improper diet. I'm afraid we overextended our credit. It's a wonder we didn't have rickets, scurvy, beri-beri or the Bluebonnet plague (from too much margarine).

I'm Coming Apart, Lord!

Different churches had different methods of feeding us. Sometimes we felt like gerbils in a cage, not knowing who would feed us or when. At some of the less contemporary places, I was asked to write a list of items I would need to cook for my family that week. Then they would cut the list in strips and pass these papers among the members. They would draw for them like the age-old custom of drawing names for Christmas. They called it a "pounding," and there were times I was sure it was aptly named.

If they didn't like their item, they would trade with someone else. If all the items didn't get selected the first time around, the "hat" was passed again. It was rather humiliating when it went into the third inning. I wanted to stand and to testify that I'd buy my own food or do without.

If, for instance, I wished to make goulash, I would write all the ingredients that went therein. Hamburger, onions, tomatoes, macaroni, chili powder. Those ingredients might go out to five different people. Part of them would remember to bring their items; the others would forget. Hence, the goo would come in and the lash wouldn't. So we'd just have goo.

Some congregations arranged to bring in food already cooked. There were times we had no inkling what we were eating. I learned early in the game, by gag order, not to let the children know if we were having fried rabbit. It was better to ask if they wanted a wing or a drumstick.

Problems showed up in as many flavorings as the food did. These volunteer cooks might bring food at any time of the day or night. It is hard for the kids' stomachs to wait. Sometimes they would "spoil their appetites" or "ruin their dinner" (as my grandmother used to say) before the meal got to the door then onto the table. It might be peas porridge hot or peas porridge cold or . . .

If a committee of women brought the meal to us dish by

A Dining Disciple

dish, it sometimes didn't match. Or mesh. Or mush. Who wants baked potatoes, scalloped potatoes, mashed potatoes and potato salad all at the same setting? Or three pies, two cakes and a batch of brownies?

I did collect some prize recipes. We stayed in one home commandeered by a gourmet chef. Goldie worked for the elite of the city. A New York chef had been bribed for a pie recipe by way of one hundred dollars under the table. Our hostess shared the recipe with me. (I only tried it once; it looked like weak mud and tasted worse.) We enjoyed souffled breads, limas extraordinaire and exotic dishes for a short period. Our adult stomachs smiled. However, the children didn't like "soup with leaves in it."

When we were fortunate enough to be picked by a prosperous church and got to go out to eat, we always overdid it. The children invariably ordered too much. Embarassed, I tried to eat mine and theirs, too. I gained thirty pounds. Cafeterias, where everything looked sublime, were the worst traps of all.

The "everybody bring something" church dinners were capital! Our stomachs laughed aloud. I'd make a lunge for the fried okra and homemade hominy, sending everyone in my wake scattering. Kevin liked the blueberry-banana pie, Angella liked macaroni and cheese and Bethany liked Jello. We were in stomach heaven.

Now and then we had a miracle. We would luck out at a church that had a running account with a grocery store, and I could buy whatever I wished! That was a rare beatitude, and I couldn't understand why more places didn't practice that practice. At such times we had "plain ole" pork chops and gravy, potatoes and green beans.

We were never poisoned, anemic or diagnosed with malnutrition. We were not sickly, bloated or hospitalized during the

I'm Coming Apart, Lord!

whole nine yards, er, years. But it wasn't our fault. The children stole cherries from the salads, raisins out of the breads and pecans off the cakes. We nibbled, ate irregularly and skipped breakfast. We had seconds and thirds that we shouldn't have eaten, rejecting firsts of others that we should have.

But most importantly, we smiled and said thank you for everything, whatever it looked or smelled or felt like. Our faces smiled, that is.

Our children have never complained from that day to this when we stop beneath the great golden arches for a hamburger. I've often wondered why, but I've never had the nerve to ask. Their stomachs might answer.

P.S. The forebegone chapter only goes to prove that one mother from the American high planes (and a bony-fried American Advantage cardholder) is capable of producing three fullblown cereal killers in a lifetime.

A Rejected Disciple

I'd heard that people made big money writing for "confession" magazines. All you had to do was confess something rather personal. I could confess to the way inflation assaulted me and send my story in. It would be *based* on truth with frequent furloughs.

I picked up my No. 2 yellow pencil. I told how my $275 electric bill put me in the state of shock, that state being the 51st in our Union. I dashed out on impulse and bought two dozen candles at $22.48 plus tax, which called for a $2.00 box of matches. That's the day I unplugged all the electrical appliances except the refrigerator.

My exaggeration got worse as I got better. I told how the hands of the wall clock stopped with sinister malice. (I liked the spooky sound of these words. They created suspense!) I rummaged in the cedar chest and came up with an old wind-up alarm clock, our first wedding gift. The fatigued alarm failed to go off the next morning, resulting in my husband's being two hours late for work. His check was docked for $23.00.

For a minimal $35.00, I purchased an antique coal oil lamp and filled it with $3.50 worth of fuel. My spouse counteracted by

I'm Coming Apart, Lord!

upping our fire insurance coverage, an additional $125.00 a month. I bought a wood-burning stove for $459.95. A cord of wood delivered cost another $135.00. An ember popped out on the carpet with the season's first cold snap, and it took $350.00 to replace the carpet.

When gasoline reached $1.50 per gallon, panic seized me. I pulled out the bicycles and dusted them off. Four new tires and tubes cost $74.00. Locks to prevent theft consumed another $18.00. Liability insurance (in case the smaller children ran over someone) was $205.00.

Wait. It gets worse. My new prohibition stated that all lights would be out after dark. That included nightlights, hall lights, porch lights and telephone lights. The oldest child overstayed his curfew one Friday night, and when the telephone rang, I panicked, darted into the darkness, stumbled over the rocking chair, hit my head on the ping-pong table and regained consciousness in the emergency room. The hospital bill was $967.00, mysteriously uncompensated by our particular policy.

The electric toaster, too, was shelved, and the pans of burned oven toast resulted in a loss of $2.70, the price of two loaves of bread.

As a conscientious inflation fighter, my most intensive efforts were directed toward shaving the food budget. Bent cans could be purchased at approximately half the retail price. On ten such items, I figured roughly a savings of $3.73. I was pleased with my thriftiness; the breadwinner would be proud of me this time.

That very evening, I needed a U-shaped can of tomato sauce for my meatloaf. The rim was somewhat distorted, and the can opener balked. I pressed down on the lever. Hard. And then harder. The $4.19 manual opener snapped, puncturing the lid at the same instant. A mighty gush of red liquid shot past my nose,

A Rejected Disciple

splattering cabinets, walls and the ceiling. The painter charged $365.00 to spot paint the ceiling and walls. My husband was furious.

Then came the unlabeled can syndrome. Unfortunately, I was racing time and government restrictions. Some bureau had just passed a law prohibiting the sale of naked cans, arguing that contents must be listed on all packaged food. That same week, I discovered a reef of unlabeled cans in a large supermarket and went so far as to ask a bright looking employee standing nearby if I might buy them. He looked at the code on the bottom, said they were tomatoes and priced them at 20 cents each with his felt marker. "Good for winter soups," I commented. He nodded nonchalantly and went back to shelving.

But when I reached the check-out counter, the clerk impolitely removed all the unclothed tins from my shopping cart. "Against the law to sell these," she cited crisply.

"But the man . . ." I stuttered helplessly.

"I can't help what the man said. There's a new law."

"But I don't care what's in the cans. We eat anything." It was almost a plea.

"I know." She softened, sliding the cans under the counter out of sight. "We do, too, but law is law."

I refused to be defeated. Remembering a small, dingy store that probably hadn't even heard about the new law yet, I raced to the backdated establishment, and sure enough, a half dozen bare cans greeted me. Triumphantly, I snatched them at a savings of 90 cents and rushed home before anyone could challenge the legality of my purchase. I had beat inflation once again!

The first can I opened was cat food. The problem was we didn't have a cat. The idea occurred to me that perhaps I could get one since throwing away the can (verily, *cans*) of cat food would be

I'm Coming Apart, Lord!

a senseless waste. When I found a "free" kitten in the classified section of the local newspaper, I complimented my good fortune. The gender of the feline went unquestioned. I named him/her Inflation. That seemed appropriate somehow.

Inflation was never beaten. To add insult to injury, he/she flatly refused the cat food and meowed for filet mignon. His/her shots cost $52.00.

The final blow that sent me into the Great Depression came the next day. I received my bank statement on the morning mail. My account was overdrawn by $0.32, and the overdraft charges overran the overwrite. A wild desperation engulfed me.

Then I remembered. The $2 bill I got for graduation. The silver certificates Grandma gave us on our anniversary. My buffalo nickels. The piggy bank that tipped its hat when you put in a quarter. Yes, it was enough to settle up. I hurried to the bank. I had won.

When I parked the car in the garage again, the sensation that someone was laughing at me was overwhelming. I glanced about suspiciously. There sat Inflation in a cool, exulting manner with a litter of six new kittens.

I ended my article here. It seemed as good a place as any. What publication wouldn't snap up such a cleverly worded masterpiece? It had all the elements of marketability: general interest subject matter, subtle suggestions for economic improvements, and a needy author.

I typed the manuscript on the old manual machine, stuffed it in the envelope and rushed it to the post office.

Then I waited in anticipation.

At 15 cents a word, I'd make a goodly sum. Would they count hyphenated words as one or two?

The manuscript came sizzling back. *Rejected!*

A Rejected Disciple

Of all the words in the dictionary, that's one of the worst. Oh, certainly, a rejection of such literary tripe is of no consequence. Nothing gained, nothing lost except postage, paper and a twenty-foot typewriter ribbon. But real rejection hurts. No pain can equal it.

You do your best, and you are rejected. You offer love, and it is rejected. You make an apology, and it is rejected. You write a letter or place a call, and your friendship is rejected.

Guess who did everything right all the time every day and was rejected? The World's Best! Jesus met grief in person and knew sorrow on a first name basis. He was badgered and battered and betrayed, but He didn't dial 911 for Heaven's EMS.

Why? So that He would know how we felt when we met our Waterloo and could carry our hurts on His shoulders. That makes being a rejected disciple a little easier, doesn't it?

A Sentimental Disciple

"How's my Dream today?" Angella climbed into the car, releasing her satchel to the mercies of the floorboard. The same question, asked each day when I picked her up from school, prefaced any other greeting or conversation. Only when she got her answer could she relax.

In 1984, a special horse entered our lives. She was a beautiful chestnut mare with a white blaze face. Her name was Dream. Perhaps the magic of memory has made her even more beautiful than she really was. Who knows?

I only saw her once, and with my limited knowledge of American quarter horses, I thought her the queenliest and bravest animal on earth. I could understand my fifteen-year-old daughter's compelling affection for her first horse, the horse she had long longed for.

After bringing Angella a few days of happiness, the special horse quietly exited our lives, leaving us sadder but richer of heart.

For years I had tried to get my husband to write, but he wasn't the sitting still type. He claimed his efforts at writing sounded like a telegram and looked like a drunk spider that had just crawled out of an inkwell and staggered across the page.

I'm Coming Apart, Lord!

I knew better. I knew his heart could write. I had a few old love letters stashed away to scotch my arguments. Sure enough, after Dream was gone, I found the account he had written about her. It was neither for publication nor for the critique of professionals; it was simply the expression of his heart. I have not edited or embellished his story. To do so would be to lose its poignancy.

She was a Dream.

She came suddenly into our lives, borne by a tragedy.

We found her in tall, dry, dead weeds and grass between a four-lane expressway and a dry, empty streambed, in a wallow made by her restless turning on wounded, sore limbs. She was really too injured to move, but we could not leave her where she would not receive proper, tender, loving care.

Struggling to her feet, she bravely responded to the call, "Come on, baby. I know it hurts, but you must come on, baby!" And come she did—through deep, dry grass and weeds that roughly raked every wound she had received by sliding down the clawing concrete embankment on her knees and side; through knee-deep mud; then into a waiting trailer; and finally to a barn, a stall, and journey's end.

For several weeks we took special care of her, fighting to save her mangled joints. She was sometimes better, sometimes worse, but mostly worse. But she was a Dream.

She had a fine head, bright eyes, and a quick mind. Why, even her registry knew she was special, for she proudly wore the name Triple's Dream. She caressed us with her nose as we, the girl and I, dressed and swabbed her wounds, but to no avail.

With eyes still alert, ears perked, head high, she met the vet who came to put her to sleep. Like a giant tree, she tumbled and was still. Over? No, it was not over. She was a Dream.

When school was out, the girl asked, first thing, "How's my Dream?"

Her daddy had to break the news, "We put her to sleep today."

"But, Daddy, I wanted to see her before she died."

"I'm sorry."

"Have they come and got her yet?"

"No. Do you want to see her?"

"Yes!" Quickly she changed into boots and jacket to protect herself against the cold, damp weather. After a quiet ride to the field, she said, "Daddy, I want to go by myself."

"Okay, honey."

Straight to her Dream she went and then knelt to caress her neck and ears. With fingers nimble and tender, she entwined her memories into the mane of her Dream. As the wind swept the girl's long hair to one side, she told her Dream goodbye.

Resolutely she turned and walked away, leaving her Dream. Once, only once, she paused to look back, drawn by some sudden call of her heart. Looking back for the last time, she advanced into the days ahead, with her Dream only in her mind.

After the remains of Dream were carried away, the aged

I'm Coming Apart, Lord!

black man, Moses Hill, called to give us the address where we were to send payment for the expenses of her removal. "Ma'am, I picked up his horse for him. But Ma'am, there was a little red ribbon tied in its mane, and a small gold pin. Ma'am, I sorta figgered it was a child what done it."

The horse was never ridden by the young girl, only loved and nursed through pain-filled, hopeless days.

Is Dream dead? No! For the girl now rides through perfect days of the mind, and verdant fields, and peaceful valleys, in places she could never have gone, in ways that could not have been—always on her Dream.

Whether in crowds amid pressure or alone in the solitude of her room, when she needs to, she saddles up, climbs up and rides away on a Dream.

"Will Dream be in Heaven, Mother?" Angella asked me.

Who was I to say that the horse wouldn't be there? Who was I to destroy a girl's Dream? When John the Revelator saw the Heavenly hosts come riding back to earth on white horses with their King, could there have been one beautiful chestnut mare with a blaze face among them?

If there happens to be one of "I, John, saw"'s horses that fits this description and if she has a scrap of red ribbon clinging to her mane, that's my daughter's Dream.

A Thinking Disciple

You have to let your children go. That's what the child psychologists tell us. Who are they trying to kid? We had to beg ours to go. And then they came boomeranging back.

Maybe it was the close proximity of the travel trailers that made them clingish. They were never more than six feet from a parent at any given time. They couldn't be–even in the bathroom. There was no place for them to play alone, cry alone or sleep alone. They had never been alone. In the grocery store or the post office or the washateria, they clung to my skirt. I looked like a Portuguese man-of-war.

Poor darlings, they couldn't run away from home like other children did. If they chose to leave, the trailer might leave while they had taken their leave, and they would be left. They didn't know their telephone number or Social Security numbers. They didn't have either or. They never knew their address to give to a policeman. Somehow, it marred their development.

They were the type of kids that might call from school, work or the mall at any given time just to check up on me to make sure I wasn't escaping.

"Mother, where were you? I let the phone ring two and

I'm Coming Apart, Lord!

one-half times...."

"I was in the bathtub."

"At this time of day? Why are you taking a bath in the middle of the afternoon?"

"I am going to the doctor."

"What do you mean trying to slip out? Why are you going to the doctor?"

"To have my arm x-rayed."

"Your arm?"

"I think it might be broken."

"What do you mean breaking your arm? You know you have to be back to cook dinner by five. We all want tacos. One of us wants flour tortillas and the other two corn. And I want black olives. Could you pick them up when you're finished at the doctor's office?"

One night after church (the aforementioned was imaginary, but this really happened), my husband and I were invited out for homemade ice cream. The couple whose house we visited were on our maturity level, and we were having a great evening filling up on fat grams. When the clock struck eleven, we were still enjoying ourselves beyond measure.

Our overgrown children called around from house to house until they found us. I was summonsed to the phone by the hostess. "Mother," the voice at the other end censured, "do you realize it is past your curfew? It's time for you to come home. Now."

I knew how Cinderella felt at midnight. We left our glass sippers and hurriedly departed, properly chastened. As we dashed the three blocks home, we hoped we weren't grounded for a month. Would our car keys be confiscated (the ultimate sentence) or our allowance axed?

Our allowance was another sore spot. Must we hand out

such a handout each week? Just for necessities? Our IRA would have to be forgotten. The budget had to be pared somewhere so the three thrillsters could have sufficient funds to buy gasoline for each of their cars. (Our son had a Corvette; we had a putrid purple pickup.) They had business to tend to. Business like going to Pizza Hut, Wal-Mart and McDonalds. We should be willing to make McSacrifices.

Any time we set up a howl, they labeled us "difficult" parents, grossly inferior to the indulgers of their peers. We were trying, we said. Indeed, we were, they agreed. Very trying.

Lately, I sense that they are beginning to doubt they will ever get us raised. And even we have our moments of despair about it. But I got to studying on all this the other day and came up with a chewing gum analogy. The more I gummed the thought, the more I knew I was on to something, some profound truth worth the chaw.

People don't chew gum like they used to. There was a time when the underside of the wooden church pews was paved with Juicy Fruit. There was even a poem about a gum-chewing girl and a cud-chewing cow being similar somehow though I've forgotten the cadence. Chewing gum was a way of life.

My parents, pre-Depression born and made of rawhide, kept chewing their gum after the sweet was gone. They put it on the bedpost at night, retrieved their ex-spearmint the next morning and chewed it until it wore out. They wouldn't think of tossing it. Get the message? If life lost its sugar coating, went flat and got hard, they plugged on year after year, never growing weary in well doing.

"Never say, 'God, I have a big problem,'" my mother used to tell me. "Say, 'Problem, I have a big God.'" Her philosophy was "when the going gets tough, tough it out."

These heavy-duty folks stuck by their principles come drought or high water. They rounded us up for family devotion

I'm Coming Apart, Lord!

each night. Dad read from the Bible, and we prayed together. Mom never sent us to school without first kneeling and praying with us before we steered our bicycles westward. But the practice of family prayer didn't stop in childhood. They plugged right on into our teenage years. When I began dating–at age 18!–my date could plan to join us in prayer if we wished to stay out later than my parents' bedtime. If I was visiting friends outside, a couple of flashes of the porch light meant, "We're ready to pray so we can turn in for the night." My friends were welcome to join us.

When we were in high school, Mom cooked a hot meal, packed it in a wooden apple crate and brought it to the city park near the school so that we could eat together. If it rained, we ate in the car, but we were together and able to say grace over the meal.

In return, I tried to be considerate of Mom. One night while I was out, sirens wailed on the highway within hearing distance of our home. I asked the young man who escorted me to drive by my house and honk the horn to let Mom know we were safe and had not been involved in an accident. I didn't want a Mom as swell as mine to lie awake and worry.

I'm afraid I've fallen short of their perfection in parenthood. My report card doesn't show all A's. Sometimes I barely pass. My generation seems a bit less durable than the previous one. Maybe even less dedicated. Oh, we chew our gum all day even after it has lost some of its flavor. But that is the limit. A new day deserves a new piece of Dentyne, however expensive.

But my kids . . . ! (Groan!) When the sugar is gone from the gum, they are through. Trash it. Why bother with month in and month out plodding? If one job, friend, church or school doesn't work out–and quickly–then get another. Theirs is a 7-Eleven, Mr. Quik culture. Easy come, easy go. Make it in the microwave. In the shower and out, and no lye soap, please. Either find the answer

A Thinking Disciple

in thirty seconds, or skip it and go on to the next question. Sometimes I wonder if the Now Generation is even passing life's tests.

But what I'm really worried about is their kids. What if they refuse to chew gum at all? What if they balk at biting down on hard things? What if they demand candy that melts in their mouths?

But that really isn't my worry. If my children ever succeed at getting me and their father out on our own, then their children can—

Oh, well. It was a nice thought.

A Doting Disciple

It's amazing what we will do for our children.

My own mother used to make pies with chocolate on one side of the pan and vanilla on the other to please everybody. We were spoiled; we were fermented.

I have known parents (no names called) to wear blisters on their feet going to parades they cared nothing about, eat at restaurants they loathed and put up crazy curtains in the den all for the love of a teenager.

We took one of ours eighty miles for harp lessons. After a year and several hundred dollars, she could play a first grade piece called "The Big Brown Bear." We could have bought a bear and had him growl in person for that amount.

My fourth grader wanted me to learn Chisenbop with her. It sounded like some sort of dance, like the Bunny Hop. Being a pastor's wife, I didn't think I ought to do it. But she said it was a new method of math in which your fingers do the dancing. I wondered if hand dancing was any less sinful than feet dancing. What mattered which extremity jitterbugged? I tried to learn the art (really) so I could speak Algebra with her. I ended up with only the algae.

I'm Coming Apart, Lord!

When a child wanted a party, he/she got one. That lesson was learned the hard way. I flatly refused to cooperate on one particular birthday. However, when gift-bearing neighbor children showed up at the door for the "party" my daughter had invited them to attend, I knew I had been tricked and had best scramble for treats. Take it straight from the horse's mouth: Fruit Loops served in Dixie cups and tap water tinctured with sugar and cake coloring will pinch-hit.

I tried to stay out of my children's car games. I was tolerant, perceptive enough to know that children cannot be styrofoam mannequins for half a million miles. But one game gave me the heebie-jeebies. It was called "The Old Gray Mare." They would count horses, but when they saw a gray one, it would cancel all the others. It reminded me of my mortality and that I wasn't what I used to be. In my early twenties, I sealed my first gray hair in an envelope and wrote the date on the outside. Now the gray proliferated. Gray mares . . . gray hairs . . . was there a connection somewhere? I was glad when they switched to the Alphabet Game or the License Plate Contest or Tic-Tac-Toe.

The school plays were such an unnecessary evil and a waste of time! I felt like a hypocrite sitting on the third row acting interested. Especially trying was "Alice in Wonderland" with a song about the "slithy toves." My body stayed put for my daughter's sake, but my mind slithered out.

I never liked varmints in the house. But if a critter was injured and the finder of the beast cried real tears, I turned a blind eye and let the animal share the room (or bed) with him or her. I never knew if the animal's wounds were real or synthetic, and I never questioned crocodile tears as long as the crocodile himself stayed at bay.

I can't believe all those weird things I bought for my

A Doting Disciple

children. Green slime. Ballpoint pens that wrapped around their arms. Toys that talked with their mouths full. Orange shoestrings that glowed in the park. Snow cones that turned their tongues blue. Why did I do it? Because they wanted them.

Therefore, when my daughter took a liking to my "parable" and asked me to include it in this book, what could a doting mother do? Dote, of course.

I named it "Happy Driving," and here it is:

Let's say that you are allotted the currency to buy one—and only one—car in your lifetime. This means you must be very careful in your choosing. You'll want one that best meets your needs not only today but on down the road.

In purchasing, you will want to remember that your vehicle's endurance is not determined by chrome and pinstriping or a pulsating stereo. Of all the cars on the lot, you wouldn't want to pick a "lemon."

You will not be allowed to get another car unless the car you buy is recalled by its manufacturer, its motor is dead and it is towed away or (heaven forbid) it is stolen from you. You cannot sell it or trade it or give it away.

Through flat tires, dry batteries, blown fuses and empty gas tanks, you must always take good care of your car so that it will run well and perform at its best. This means you will not abuse the vehicle in any way: no peeling out or high speed chases or careless driving.

As much as possible, you must avoid side roads with potholes, flying rocks and debris that might damage the car. You must drive with caution so as not to dent or scratch it.

I'm Coming Apart, Lord!

You will not want the interior to become shabby through neglect, either. Attention to small problems when they first appear saves major repair bills later. A carport or garage is advisable to safeguard the car in bad weather.

Knowing that you cannot trade for a newer or fancier model, it is useless, yea, even foolish to stop by the new car dealers or pore over enticing brochures that might tempt you to want to exchange your present vehicle for a different model since you have not been given the currency to buy or trade for another.

To protect your car from theft, you should keep the key to your car in your pocket, never leave it unlocked to vandals, do not park it where it will appear to be abandoned, and install a good alarm system that screams, "This is my car. Bug off!"

When you are out of town on a trip or on your job or with friends and you spot a car that looks better than your own, remember that you have a car that still runs. You chose it. You bought it. You signed a contract on it.

Even if you find a very attractive automobile sitting by the curb with the keys left in the ignition, you must not take it even for a short trial drive around the block and back again. It does not belong to you; it is not your property. That is stealing.

Always drive courteously. With proper maintenance, your car will see you through a lot of miles, up hill and down.

Many happy years of driving for you and the car you purchased!

A Doting Disciple

Since this is a parable of your marriage, you might want to read it over again.

A Happy Disciple

My husband and I never had a date. He proposed over the Bell telephone, and I got ready for wedding bells.

Five years before my body started traveling with him, my heart went. It followed him everywhere, and I hoped it might haunt him.

It didn't. He scarcely knew I existed.

"I just feel like I'm going to marry Elroy Martin, and there's not a thing I can do about it," I told my mother as I swung my seventeen-year-old legs off the side of the bed. It was a ludicrous idea. Competition for single preachers was worse than the lineup at a 90% off, going out of business sale.

At least a dozen eligibles were after Elroy Martin. The mention of his name brought swoons. One young lady resorted to tucking an onion in her handkerchief so she could "weep" at prayer time, leaving the impression she was "spiritual." Another requested herself to sing so that she could traipse in front of him on the way to the platform. I just put callouses on my knees.

I knew little about the man, but that didn't matter. My third eye told me he would be worth more than the prayers it cost me to

I'm Coming Apart, Lord!

get him. But I was over six feet tall, freckled faced and (let's face it) no beauty queen. What hope did I have with the blue-eyed hunk of masculinity two thousand miles away?

The long arm of coincidence is sometimes very startling. Elroy and I were born in the same county, a block apart, a year apart. Romantically, our birth certificates shared the same filing cabinet in the Bosque County Courthouse. But before my first birthday, our ways parted, and over the years, our paths seldom crossed. I remember every sighting of him; he remembers almost none of them.

Just graduated from Plainview High School, he came with his dad to help build our new church building in Cleburne, Texas. My heart did flipflops!

My brother, Bobby, established a friendship with Elroy. Through illegal bribes, I kept Bobby corresponding with him, composing the letters myself. But space between them grew wider and wider with time and other interests.

Months passed. I finished high school and needed direction for my life. Dad had an underground prayer room beneath his study. I borrowed this damp, musty concrete square for a talk with God. I needed a concrete answer.

"Now, Lord," I prayed, never more sincere, "I want to know for sure that this is the man for me. You know there's a convention going on in Dallas. You know I'm going to that convention. If he is the one I'm to marry, get him there!"

It was a big order. Elroy hadn't planned to be in Dallas at all. En route to New Mexico, Dallas was out of his way. But a friend suggested they stop by the conference for one night, and Elroy delayed catching his bus until the next day.

That night, my family and I were there, and Dad (bless him!) offered Elroy a ride as far as Cleburne, several miles closer to his

A Happy Disciple

destination, and a night's lodging. My well-trained brother inconspicuously seated Elroy in the back seat with me, and I almost died of a runaway pulse! Here I was sitting beside the man I was going to marry, and he didn't even know I was going to marry him! (By the way, absolutely nothing romantic happened except for the candy he shared with me.)

The Greyhound bus took him away.

We girls had a crazy game going that summer. Merely kids' stuff, it resulted in many a good laugh. We counted one hundred red convertibles, then located a woman wearing an orchid suit and finally looked for a man wearing a solid green necktie. The next guy we saw would be our groom.

It took a while to fill that prescription, but I was down to the tie. I spotted it! It was bright green and entwined a man's neck in Abilene, Texas. Standing beside that man was Elroy Martin. He was visiting his brother who had just moved there.

Then when I was nineteen, I heard he was engaged to be married. I had some strong questions for God. "If he's mine, Lord, why is he marrying someone else?" Nothing made sense. I bombarded Heaven with such agonizing pleas that the angels must have used a whole box of Kleenex sopping up their tears for me. Soon afterward, I heard he was unengaged. I think even the angels were relieved.

My "Jonah" then took off to a far country. I lost him somewhere in California for two years. By now, I was twenty-one and worried about being a spinster. My patience gave out like poor Sarah's in the Bible, and I started dating local Christian boys. "A bird in the hand is worth two in the bush," logic said. After all, this Mr. Martin had shown me no personal attention by letter, phone or in person. Ever.

When I came in from a date one night, having promised

I'm Coming Apart, Lord!

myself and the young man with whom I was "going steady" that I would come to some conclusion about our future, I reached for my well-used "promise box." Shaped like a loaf of bread, it was full of scripture cards. As per my habit, I pulled one and read it. The words leaped at me: "WAIT, I say, on the Lord. . . ." I looked around. Had God spoken aloud I wouldn't have been more surprised!

Elroy's twenty-second birthday was coming up, and I decided to send him a card. I had nothing to lose. I didn't even know his address, but I had heard that he was in the San Diego area. I sent the greeting in care of the pastor there, and he passed it on.

It read, "Almost missed your birthday; the thought makes me squirm. In fact, to put it truthfully, I feel just like a worm!" When the card was opened, a spring, painted like a worm, popped out. I penned in, "Hey, man, you're gettin' old," and signed my name. It was April, 1958.

God had already started working across the California border. Elroy's cousin there had just lost his girlfriend and was having withdrawals. "Say, I got a card today from this girl back in Texas. . . ." He proceeded to tell his cousin every nice thing he could remember about me.

The cousin answered, "That sounds fine, but she is two thousand miles from here," and dropped the subject.

Back in his bachelor's apartment, Elroy began to think–or the Lord began to talk. *Now, if that girl back in Texas is everything I told my cousin she is, then why don't I write to her myself?* He didn't realize his thinking was being prompted by some stiff eastward prayers. He sat down and wrote me a friendly letter before the week was out.

The letter made one small stipulation. "If you are not writing or keeping company with any young man, I would like to

A Happy Disciple

make this the beginning of our communication," he said. If I was involved with someone else, he stressed, he would not pursue the friendship.

A personal commitment saved my life! Our church was in revival, and I had made it a policy not to date anyone during revivals. "I want to stay and pray as long as I wish," I told my male friends. "There will be no dating until the revival ends." I broke all ties, curtailed all social life and put my whole self into the services. The letter from Elroy arrived one day before the revival closed. I could honestly say I was dating no one. Again, God's timing was perfect! However, on June 23, my mom's and dad's silver anniversary, he broke off the correspondence. He wrote that he didn't think we were made for each other. No further explanation.

I fell apart. I cried. I fasted. Cornelius' prayers could not hold a light to mine. Every morning when the Lord got up, the first thing He saw was a great hump in Heaven's floor where my prayers were pushing up through the clouds.

I was expecting my sweetheart's call the afternoon it came. It was the first time he had ever called me. Dad must have suspected something, too; he picked up the extension phone. While Elroy was proposing, Dad was writing as fast as the pencil would move, trying to get it down in black and white.

That unnotarized document, now in my possession, is numbered from one to twenty-four. There are twenty-three "he said"s and one "she said." The one "she said" was number seventeen. Most of the sentences are maddeningly incomplete, but here's a sampling:

    2. I decided . . . there's nobody but you.
   11. I always . . .
   14. I can talk this out with Brother Gray. (His pastor)

I'm Coming Apart, Lord!

16. Would you . . . have me as your husband . . . ?
17. Okay. (LaJoyce)
18. You . . .
20. . . . I'm real happy, how about you?
21. We . . . get together on something soon.
23. I want to . . .
24. <u>I really love you</u>. Bye. (Last words.)

When I hung up the telephone, I was engaged to be married to the man of my dreams. I was so excited I remembered very little of the conversation. But it didn't matter; he was mine. *Mine!*

"Did I get a letter today, Mom?" That was my daily question for the next eleven months. He wrote to me almost every day. Phone calls were too expensive for his $40 per week wages.

He returned from California only once, riding the bus for three days and three nights to meet me at the Amarillo camp meeting. Because his bus was delayed, we had less than an hour together there.

However, my brother drove me four hundred miles to hear him preach one night. He made the return trip with us then left the next day for the West Coast. As he departed, he tossed his handkerchief out the window to me. Now I had something tangible! A dirty handkerchief! I still have it.

Some of our love letters, stored under a hot water tank, were destroyed by moisture. One that remains was dated March, 1959. He asked how soon after May 1 I could be ready for the wedding. My reply, dated March 23, says, "Fifteen minutes past midnight of May 1st!"

On Saturday, May 16, he arrived at my house at 6:30 p.m., forgetting that he was scheduled to preach in Hillsboro, thirty miles away, that evening. I went with him, and the small church took up

A Happy Disciple

a collection for us, our first. Elroy gave me the pennies. Those six copper colored wheat coins live in my wedding book.

We were married six days later on Friday, May 22, 1959. I bought the marriage license myself.

The wedding was every ounce as wild as the courtship. Tornado clouds skipped about town, shutting off the electricity in the northern section of the city. We delayed the ceremony a half hour, waiting for the attendants to get through the storm. Two groomsmen did not show up at all.

It rained torrents. The lawn, designated for our reception, disappeared under an inch of water. I pulled off my white shoes, gathered my floor-length wedding dress (that hid my calloused knees!) about me and waded the river to the church.

I sailed through the "I do"s and "I will"s then dropped my bride's bouquet right in front of everybody. With one grand swoop, I retrieved it and swished down the aisle toward the exit. At the reception, a large miller bug dived into the punch and swam the full length of the bowl.

Most brides would have been in a frenzy of tears by this time, but not I! I had waited five years for this moment, shed enough tears to float a battleship, and no amount of tribulation could mar my newfound happiness. I smiled all the way through! I was looking forward to our first date.

We had $35 for a honeymoon, but God took care of that, too. A family friend, proprietress of a motel/restaurant near Texarkana, promised, "When you two get married, I'll give you my best room." The food from her grill was "on the house."

On Sunday, we attended church where a revival was in progress. The pastor asked us to sing. Our first song was "Nothing Can Compare," and our second "It Was A Miracle." Back at the room, we howled with laughter. We enjoyed our singing so much

I'm Coming Apart, Lord!

that we went back every night of our honeymoon. The last evening, my husband gave away our secret, we were a newly Mr. and Mrs.

The magnolia trees were in magnificent bloom. We fished, picked wild plums and painted "Tom Sawyer" and "Becky Thatcher" on our straw hats.

"I didn't have a chance," my husband tells me. "You went to a Higher Power!" And that is exactly what I did.

There were occasions when I thought death would "do us part," but for better or for worse, we robbed the hearse. It is hard to believe our silver wedding anniversary has come and gone. Now we are going for gold–whether it be May 22, 2009, or in Heaven.

A Protected Disciple

My sister-in-law and I believe in angels. Neither of us have seen one, but we are sure they've seen us. A little too often. We hope their wings aren't sprung from running interference for us and our offspring.

JoAnne and I had a grand total of seven children, which is supposed to be a number symbolic of perfection, something our seven were seven antonyms of.

She will tell you of a time when she had her back turned for milliseconds, and that was an hour too long. She heard a dreadful screech of tires and the blare of a car horn. Without waiting for spurs, her legs took off running.

She lived a few yards off busy Highway 67, and sure enough, her third child, three-year-old Kendall, had joined the traffic on his tricycle. He was in the wrong lane and had trumped up a four-way stop where there was no intersection.

"Lady!" a man stuck his head out the side window of his car. "Don't you ever watch your kid?"

Watch him? she thought. *That's all I ever do!*

With the fourth baby on its way, she needed extra hands, extra eyes and extra angels.

I'm Coming Apart, Lord!

Kendall seemed bent on self-destruction. He kept his angel in overdrive. His mother found him bouncing up and down on the lid of an abandoned well he had found on the property. The lid was split, webbed with a network of hairline cracks over its entire surface. She vows the angel held it together until she got there to rescue him.

Then there was the time he fell headlong into the church bapistry while she and her husband were cleaning the church. Above the whirr of the sweeper, an inner ear picked up the splash she heard in the distance, and she screamed, "Kendall has fallen into the bapistry!"

Her husband hopscotched along the backs of the pews, leaped to the tank and fished out his soggy son who lay on the bottom holding his breath. Or was his angel holding his nose?

After that experience, JoAnne drew a mental picture of Kendall's angel: snow white hair, furrowed brows, and haggard, pleading with God to assign someone else to that incorrigible tad. How many hours of overtime can one angel be expected to work?

"He needed a fresh angel every morning!" she laughed.

JoAnne's stories are goosebumpers, but I've had some firsthand encounters myself. While my husband worked at a camp for teens one summer, I needed to get myself into town via a thriving highway that led to Houston. I have never won any driving trophies; I'm terrified of traffic, and they're terrified of me. But it was too far to walk. Or run. Or crawl.

"Now, Lord," I prayed, "just this once, I need angels on that expressway to stop all the traffic so I can get out on the highway to go to the motel."

When I got to the intersection of the swarming, never still four lanes, I looked this way and that. There wasn't a car in sight. The angels had put up barricades! I was afraid to tell anyone, afraid

A Protected Disciple

that no one would believe me.

North of Colorado Springs on a black midnight, we topped a mountain doing sixty miles an hour. Warm-blooded southerners, we weren't familiar with Colorado's winter quirks. We were traveling on a sheet of ice and didn't know it. Just beyond the crest of the mountain, the road bore to the left. When my driver husband turned the steering wheel to follow the road, nothing happened.

The car went straight on, edging closer and closer to the right shoulder where there were no guardrails. If we plunged off, we would fall hundreds of feet, vanish like the Sears catalogue and be found next spring. It looked like doomsday for us. We were going off the road, prisoners of a vehicle headed for certain disaster.

Realizing our plight, we made a mighty verbal cry to God to rescue us. Suddenly, something began to push the car back on the road, opposing all inertial forces. "They" pushed us all the way to the inside lane next to the median. I've always wondered how many angels that feat took.

By now we were going 70 . . . 75 . . . and then 80 toward the bottom of the mountain and a bustling truck stop where trucks came and went like Solomon's ships from Tarshish.

Not a truck budged as we whizzed by at 85 miles an hour. The angels held them all in position on the ramp until our wheels found dry ground again.

When we settled down from our travels, we needed a second car. A gentleman in Arkansas offered us a nice little back model Corvair. It was parked in his yard two hundred miles away, and he said it was ours for the coming after.

It fell my lot to drive it home. The temperature was well below freezing, but we checked and found that the heater worked well. I was grateful for that.

However, when I rolled down the window to give a last

I'm Coming Apart, Lord!

thanks to our benefactor, to my chagrin, it wouldn't roll up again. The donor said he'd never had problems with it before. It had worked perfectly until this moment!

I pounded and yanked. I jerked the handle clockwise and counterclockwise. But it would not budge. It would only go up so far, stopping about halfway. No amount of coaxing could get it to go any farther.

We were on a limited time schedule and couldn't wait for repairs. I buttoned up my coat, put on gloves and a scarf and still very nearly froze in that two hundred mile stretch. The heater couldn't hope to win against all that outside air straight from the North Pole. Now and then along the way, I tried to get the window to cooperate. Nothing doing.

When I drove into my own driveway and turned off the motor, I reached for the window crank without thinking. It rolled up as smoothly as if it had been greased with Dippity-Do.

My husband checked the car. The heater received its heat from around the exhaust manifold. The manifold had a leak, sending carbon monoxide directly into the cab with me. Had the car been airtight, I would have been in big trouble, asphyxiated, for instance. But I was a protected disciple that day.

. . . And to think I tried to shut the window on that poor angel's hand!

That might constitute angel abuse.

A Faithful Disciple

This chapter isn't about me and mine. It's about a fellow disciple. A firm, fadeless, fervent, focused, forthright, forgiving and faithful one.

We looked for switchbacks on the half million mile highway that would take us by Uncle Dutch's place. During our years of travel, we stopped in several times.

He was an authentic country preacher, weather beaten but never beaten. He stood square shouldered and shot straight. I hated to lose such a pearl-handled man, and I miss him yet.

He had a primitive church in the "sticks." It was primitive to the tune of no plumbing. Once an open arbor, the listing framework had been boxed in and stood proudly out of hoyle on a hill. Uncle Dutch didn't even have running water in his home unless he ran for it himself.

"My salary is $500 a month," Uncle would chuckle. "Fifty dollars in cash and four hundred and fifty in peace and quiet." His farmer members brought him turnip greens and hog jowl. He did a lot of fishing without license, accompanied by Nicodemus, a stray dog he had adopted.

I had thirty-four immediate aunts and uncles (spouses

I'm Coming Apart, Lord!

included) scattered from Dan to Beersheba. Not going past once removed, at least ten of these were preachers of various denominations. Uncle Dutch was one of the best of the lot besides being one of the most unique.

Uncle Dutch never talked much about himself. Orphaned a few days after birth, his childhood was splattered with the graffiti of neglect and loneliness. Shunted from household to household, he felt unwanted and miserable. A misfit. At a young age, he'd been clipped from life's happily ever after stories by misfortune's scissors.

When his oldest brother was murdered, leaving a widow and two tots, Dutch listened to the pros and cons of the stabbing. He formed his own verdict, and a tormenting revenge rankled in him. When the murderer was not convicted, he grew angry. Now it became his sole responsibility to settle the score.

He followed itinerant jobs for several months, and when he returned to his hometown, someone invited him to a revival "upstairs in the old feed store building." Here he was welcomed and treated as a friend; he returned the next night.

The parson opened his tattered Bible. As the wind ruffled the pages, he read, "Dearly beloved, avenge not yourselves, but rather give place to wrath; for it is written, Vengeance is mine, I will repay, saith the Lord." (Romans 12:19) Who had told the minister about his plans for revenge? How did he know?

He had heard that a little book was kept in the pulpit with names for whom these devoted people were praying. He had to see that book! The following night, he mingled among them, working his way toward the front. He saw the list with his own name toward the top, and it touched him profoundly. Soon afterward, he gave his life to God.

Then he faced the supreme test. One night as he looked over the congregation, he spotted the man who had killed his

A Faithful Disciple

brother, the man for whom he had carried the torch of revenge for so long. The inner battle raged, and how his Pharaoh pursued him! The murderer went to the front and knelt at the altar. Dutch rose from his seat, made his way to the mourner's bench, put his arms around his enemy and prayed for him. Born in Dutch that night was a desire to help fallen humanity find the peace with God that he had found.

He bought a cheap guitar and practiced with grim determination until he mastered the basic chords of G, D and C. Then he journeyed about, singing with such sincerity that he was received everywhere.

His faith grew, too. When a group of gospel workers needed food, he prayed. As the bread truck rounded the corner at the intersection, a loaf of bread tumbled off and rolled right toward him!

Uncle Dutch married my mother's younger sister, Adele, and they had four children. One of their sons followed the wrong crowd. But a mother's prayers chased him in and out of trouble.

The gang the boy had joined planned a bank robbery. He was appointed as the driver of the getaway car. He wouldn't have to go into the bank, steal anything or hurt anybody, they said. It was a cake job. He agreed to help.

On the day of the robbery, his mother spent hours in prayer, feeling a particular heaviness. Where was her son, and what was the problem?

At the last minute, the boy went to the gang members. "I can't go," he said. When they pressed him for a reason, he just shook his head and held to his decision. That day, he had heard his mother's voice as she prayed, and he was many miles from her.

The robbery went off as planned, netting a big pot to divvy up. Everything went well until the fleeing vehicle pulled away from

I'm Coming Apart, Lord!

the curb. The police opened a barrage of gunfire, and the substitute driver was struck in the head and killed.

Uncle Dutch was a friend to the friendless, with a heart "as big as a No. 3 washtub." His crowning moment began with the call to visit Hulen. Hulen was in the County jail awaiting trial. In a fit of jealousy, he had bludgeoned his wife with a piece of pipe. He admitted to the deed and showed genuine remorse. There were no traces of bitterness or strands of malice in the man. He was quiet, well-mannered, friendly and looked more like a doctor than a convict. In court, Hulen was given the death penalty.

Uncle Dutch fought valiantly, appearing before the Board of Pardons and Paroles, asking that the sentence be reduced to life in prison. He prayed for a miracle.

The chaplain and the warden of the State penitentiary said Hulen was the best prisoner they had ever had. He had obtained his pardon from an unseen Judge, they agreed. His execution date was set.

When Uncle Dutch learned that Hulen would be alone for "the last mile," he couldn't bear the thought. He decided to go with him to the electric chair. He slept very little from that moment. He tossed. He cried. He prayed. He couldn't eat. It wouldn't be like watching a stranger die; Hulen had become his personal friend.

The brave parson entered the death room a few minutes ahead of Hulen. He had prayer with the condemned man before they strapped him into the chair. "May God bless everyone," Hulen said, and the muffled sounds of worship could be heard from beneath the hood. Uncle Dutch stood directly in front of him and braced for the shock. Hulen wouldn't feel it, but his friend would–now and perhaps for the rest of his life.

The miracle came but in a much different way than Uncle Dutch expected. Before the shock hit his body, Hulen's skin turned

A Faithful Disciple

a deep purple. Prison officials said he was already gone when the jolt came. The prison physician said Hulen may have "fainted" as indicated by the blood rushing to the surface of his body. An editor and veteran reporter of the newspaper who had covered more than a hundred executions said he had never witnessed anything like it.

Headlines of the *Globe Times* blazed this question: WAS HULEN DEAD WHEN THE CURRENT STRUCK HIM? AUTHORITIES WONDER.

The faithful disciple turned to walk away. He had gone the last mile with his friend, Hulen. But so had Someone Else.

A Weary Disciple

Our travel trailer hunkered in my father-in-law's blackberry patch as weary as I. From the first day of January until the middle of August, we'd had a total of eleven nights off. With two services on Sunday, that averaged 1.009 services a day. We had been traveling for 9.3 years and needed to cool our heels. We were ragged out body, soul and wardrobe.

If we don't close soon, we'll soon be out of clothes, I thought.

The children were emerging from the small stage to the tall stage. The cycle of laundries, home schooling and garment alterations gave me the sensation that I was caught in a revolving door. As I mended the ravels and rips, I wondered if I might be unraveling myself while I ripped about trying to get everything done. There weren't enough hours in the day anymore.

We held a few nights' worth of services at the folks' church while we occupied their berry plot. We made a woeful flop. "If you can't beat this, you won't have invitations long," my mother-in-law said to me. She had always been forthright with me, and I knew that what she said was the gospel truth without a polygraph to prove it. But by the time I got to church each night, I felt like a

I'm Coming Apart, Lord!

tractor with the deferential stripped out. I shiver to think what I looked like.

In the garden, I slept like a baby. Two hours of sleep, an hour of crying, etc. It was time for a change.

But where? When? How? We waited and prayed and prayed and waited. As badly as I wanted a change, I feared changes. I was accustomed to wheels and miles and my #2 yellow pencil. What would I do with flower beds and a mailbox and (the unthinkable) an electric typewriter with its own moods?

Then we got a call about a new church that had just opened on the hem of the central Texas metroplex. It had little to offer but an opportunity. We snatched it! I think we accepted the invitation more out of desperation than a burden.

We uprooted the tired trailer, crossed over Leon River and found a place to park in a shabby space near the downtown area of the city. It was the cheapest trailer park in town; at $35 a month, it was woefully overpriced. The trailers were packed in neck to neck. Avenue H, where they were located, didn't stand for Heaven, but it could have stood for horrible. It was a dreadful place.

We awoke each morning to the curses of the woman parked behind us. She swore at the weather, her children or anything that moved. One day I heard my four-year-old in the bathroom spanking her doll. She was shouting, "Cuss word! Cuss word! Cuss word!" at the poor plastic baby. I knew it was time for me to pray us out of there.

Two school authorities came to ask why the nine-year-old wasn't in public school. I showed them his correspondence course and assured them that I would gladly enroll him as soon as we had a permanent address and I knew where he should go.

We hadn't been there but a few days when the tree trimmers came and killed every tree near us. The only scenery left was beat-

A Weary Disciple

up garbage cans.

Our search for a lot on which to build a home led us to a wonderful tree-studded location in a swanky part of town. At a point where two roads met, the lot had five sides. To build a house that met all the city regulations on this five-angled haven seemed impossible. That's why it was cheap and still unsold, no doubt. We worked and cried and prayed over a floorplan large enough to house us. We finally succeeded in drawing one that passed city inspection.

We would sit in the car on our house site and look at the miniature forest of trees. There were hackberry and white oaks in abundance. But "our tree" was the mighty post oak that towered thirty-five feet into the sky. That one, we decided, full-limbed and majestic, would stand near our front door. While we were putting down roots, it would be a silent sentinel, the epitome of constancy. Our Rock of Gibraltar.

One day I picked up my #2 yellow pencil and wrote a prayer inspired by the oak tree, so parallel to the metamorphosis my life had undergone:

>Dear God,
>I watched the massive oak tree near my window
>>all winter long
>>>and was surprised.
>
>Surprised that it wore the same clothes
>>through frost and cold.
>
>The other trees put off their garments and
>>shivered,
>>>but not the oak.
>
>The wind shrieked, shaking its branches;
>>still the foliage held on tightly.

I'm Coming Apart, Lord!

The decade's worst storm unfurled,
    but the leaves doggedly clung,
        never giving up.
This is so much like myself, Lord.
Struggling to hold on through the season of
    bitter trial,
Refusing to relinquish the known,
    the visible;
        there's security in sameness.
For who wants to be bare. . . .
Exposed to painful circumstances . . .
    stripped of resources?
So I refused to give up my old leaves
    even in the storm.
But as I watched the oak out my window,
    spring came.
One morning the leaves turned loose willingly
    and plummeted to the ground,
        defeated,
Turned loose of their own accord without
    wind or force.
    The change came in one day.
        All at once.
I went to see what had happened because
    I was surprised.
The tree was bare. Bare and waiting . . .
I found that new life, surging up in the tree,
    coaxed the old to let go

A Weary Disciple

      when nothing else could.
Lord, You have a lesson in this oak for me.
   A paradox
Of old haunts that cling stubbornly
   to our lives
      out of the past, refusing to drop.
Storms of tears and winds of fate
   never faze them.
Same worn path, unchanged;
   we weary of our thoughts
      we cannot shed.
Then, amazing discovery,
   we awaken to a new horizon,
      surprised that winter leaves are gone.
Crowded out by new inspirations,
   full of faith and hope.
      All at once, the change has come.
Thank you, Lord, for the timely message.
   Now I understand that there's
   no need for fear.
Every life passes through its bleak,
   cold days,
      but beauty waits to clothe that life.
The bareness is but for a span, at winter's end . . .
   in preparation for the new.
When I turn loose and feel
   my cast disclosed,
      with a peaceful calm, I can say

I'm Coming Apart, Lord!

HALLELUJAH!
Spring cometh to my soul!

A Runaway Disciple

I'd been married fifteen years and had never lived in a house. The two short-term mobile homes we had before and between the travel trailers were only eight feet widers. Stretched out in them, I was a wall to wall person.

But at last, we would have a home! The children, who had never had a room of their own, would own a room. I could have real glass plates instead of Melmac. The door facings would be tall enough and wide enough so that when I passed through, I wouldn't rearrange my hairdo or my hips. No hardship seemed too great while I waited in anticipation for my home. It was akin to waiting for that first baby.

The problem was that my husband worked from daylight until dark–from "can" to "can't"–on the house, and there was no paycheck. We tightened our belts until we were gasping for something besides air.

Fortunately, Krogers had a chronic sale going. We ate their nickel cans of biscuits for six weeks. My nine-year-old ate twenty at one setting, a whole dime's worth. We had no meat at all. When someone gave us an aged hen, we could have cackled for joy, and we picked her bones clean. I've forgotten where I obtained the coffee can filled with bacon grease, but it made wonderful gravy. Water gravy isn't half bad.

Construction on the house began in late September. Winter was coming, our first in the expando trailer. We didn't know how well insulated it was. We learned. It wasn't. Sleet and snow sifted in the crack where the two parts fit together. The children and I were miserably cold, and I feared that one of them would take pneumonia if it didn't take them first. We had no health insurance, and if there was such a thing as Medicaid then, we didn't know about it.

By January, the house was finished except for the outside brick and the fireplace. "Why can't we go ahead and move in and finish it later?" I questioned. "At least we'd be warm."

"Because the city inspector won't let us."

"Who is this city inspector, and why won't he let us?"

"He's very hard-nosed. The brick must be on before he'll green tag the meter boxes."

"The children are freezing. What is the man's name? Who do I call?"

"It won't do any good. He won't budge."

I knew a God that could budge Mr. Hardnose. I was God's child, and we were as cold as lizards. There was a warm house in a lovely neighborhood ready for me and my children, except for some minor details like brick. I had a talk with God about the talk I planned with the city inspector. Then I picked up the telephone and called him. He said, yes, ma'am, he'd be right out to green-tag the house for me, and I could move in.

I didn't waste any time. I moved in, less furniture. With naught to mellow the spaciousness, the rooms looked like Carlsbad Caverns. I feared that I or one of the children might get lost in the chambers of the building. It seemed awesomely large to me

A Runaway Disciple

although at 1664 feet of living area it was probably the smallest house in the suburb.

"If you find me huddled in the wash room, you'll know that I'm terrified of so much space," I told my husband. I wandered about in my bathrobe, trying to get my bearings. We might need a trolley to get from one end of the house to the other.

We went to buy beds and were just getting them assembled when our first "batch" of company showed up: a cousin, his wife and their eighteen-month-old baby. Our first guests! We were delighted. They stayed three days, returned to Houston for their belongings and came back to help us get a church started. The girls wagged the baby around like a rag doll, filling his diaper with sand. During the next five years, this family was an anchor in the storm for us.

The next visitors stayed for two weeks. Newlyweds, they camped in our recreation room until their apartment came open. They moved part of their stuff and left part of it behind.

With a heart for homeless and hurting people, our house gradually began to fill with such. A wanderer moved in and brought his son. A seventeen-year-old whose parents were both hospitalized joined us. She lived with us for several years as dear as our own daughter. Young men from a nearby army base made our home their home away from home. They came on weekend passes. As the weeks passed, there were more and more passers. Three of the church adopted us when gales blew up a tempest at their own home. We couldn't seem to turn a deaf door to anyone.

Then the people who came and went began to invite their own families and friends in for visits. I had yeast bread rising almost around the clock. I cooked endlessly. For a while, it was fun. Then I got fed up with feeding the unfed world.

When I'd had enough, I weeded my own children from the

I'm Coming Apart, Lord!

melee. Miraculously, I still remembered which three they were. "Pack a duffel bag and drop it out your window," I hissed. "We're running away from home!"

They did as they were instructed, and their father slipped behind the house to gather their knapsacks. Unnoticed, we stole out the back door and quietly sped away.

We had a marvelous time at the lake, swimming and splashing and picnicking. I forgot about cooking, stretching the budget or cleaning mildew off the shower curtains. When we returned to the crowd at home, as far as I could discern, no one had even missed us. They went right on enjoying our lovely house, eating leftovers. For years afterward, the children talked about "the time we ran away from home."

I think it taught us all something. When the problems just won't go away, it helps if we leave them for a while. Oh, certainly, they will still be there when we get back. And maybe they won't even miss us. But just maybe we'll see them through different eyes, eyes that have seen the blue of a lake, the evening sunset and sailboats.

Try it sometime.

A Hurting Disciple

"Have a nice time, honey." My husband kissed me goodbye. The kiss needed a three-week shelf life. I hoped it didn't expire before then.

I was just short of being comatose when I set out on that unforgettable trip. Never, never should I have gone to the Never, Never Land without my better half. But he had been in a wreck–he'd had a Big Mac attack, meeting a truck head-on–and wasn't able to travel. My friend, Carole, offered to go in his stead.

The day I went out my front door, my back decided to go out, too, with a ruptured disk. I wasn't able to travel either, but I did.

At the airport, I discovered I had left my overnight case with my most essential essentials at home an hour back in history. I hoped Carole would have enough deodorant, toothpaste and hairspray for both of us. But, perish the thought, my pain pills were in that case. I knew I'd miss my plane if I backpedaled.

As I limped toward the concourse, my daughter galloped up, red-faced and harried. With her hair all askew, she'd never looked as pretty. "Here's the bag you forgot, Mother." She'd found the luggage sitting on my bed and broke the sound barrier in a 1982

I'm Coming Apart, Lord!

Chevrolet truck to get it to me before my plane departed. I have loved Chevys and bad hair days ever since.

The lousy start should have been warning enough even before the green noodles and hut-shaped pretzels the airline served. I would have thought I was hallucinating, but the pasta looked green to Carole, too.

Well, let's back up. Actually, the passport ID would have been red flags for a lucid person. They had taken two shots. In the first picture, I looked like warmed-over death. In the second, I wasn't even warmed over. According to the photos, either I was too sick to make this trip, or I desperately needed an outing.

In San Francisco, I got cold feet about leaving the United States with the screaming sciatica and called my husband. "I want to come home. I'm hurting." I cried real tears, sorry they couldn't drip through the phone line. "Please."

"No, you've gone that far, and you'll make it," he coached. "You're sure to be a blessing over there. Trust God, and go on." He had never believed God's plans had a reverse gear and had no pity that I was stuck in low.

By the time I got to Hawaii, I was wheelchair material. Carole pushed me to and fro, and a friend showed us around the island. With the pain, nothing was plain. I didn't care about sunken ships, crowded beaches or pineapple. The souvenirs I bought were made in Hong Kong. (I forgot to look on the bottom.)

Life got more blurry with time and with medication. The two-story, all-night Australian airship provided gray socks for all passengers. They didn't help my backache any. I couldn't concentrate on the Celsius temperature on the screen. Going from summer to winter with such speed, one wouldn't have time to get his coat from the cleaners. When we crossed the International Date Line, I got confused and couldn't decide whether I was a day younger or

A Hurting Disciple

a day older.

The hostess served wonderful food, but I didn't know what it was. The Cold Collation on the menu sounded too much like coalition to me, and I was afraid the Baba would talk back. The Ling and Black Butter didn't sound bad albeit a little frightening. Some sort of muesli greeted me from my breakfast tray. "I think it was Mussolini," I confessed to someone. I never did get what I asked for to drink, but it was probably for the best. Water was a safe compromise.

When we got to Sydney, I thought everyone was driving on the wrong side of the road. With the steering wheels on backward, manuevering was like a nightmare. The Australian word for wreck is "prang," and I was a nervous prang every time I got in the car.

The first night there, I lay in bed with my camera, taking pictures of pictures on the wall while Carole went to see the oversized celery. The four hours between pain pills seemed like four centuries. Sometimes I took them two at a time to survive. (I took the pills, not the centuries.)

As guest speaker for the New South Wales Women's Retreat, I sat on a bar stool, balanced myself behind the podium, pointed my nose toward the microphone and hoped I made sense. The in-house staff furnished me with codeine pills.

It was July, and ice frosted the car windows every morning. I knew it wasn't an illusion because I wasn't the only one who noticed it. I watched a man scrape his windshield. I was relieved that he had seen it, too, and that I wasn't imagining things.

My second leg took me to Queensland. Special friends, Roscoe and Mary Seay, lived there. Mary saw my plight and took me to a doctor immediately. He prescribed even more pills. With the added medication, I was able to see koala bears, kangaroos and the Great Barrier Reef. The ocean floor, vague through the murky

I'm Coming Apart, Lord!

mini-submarine windows, was an apt metaphor of my fuzzy mind. I agreed with Apostle Paul that I was seeing through a glass darkly.

At market I ate crocodile sausage. The Darvocet helped to take my mind off what I was eating. We bought handkerchiefs with maps of the continent in silhouette for our friends back home. With a little mispronunciation, they became silly-wets. The 132 foot bungee jump didn't even scare me, but I didn't jump. I purchased a didgeridoo, the only musical instrument played by the aborigines. These bugles are crafted by termites from a tree limb. I bought mine from a native, but I must have picked up the exterminator's tab, too. I tried to blow on/in it, but the bellow that came forth resembled a moose with laryngitis.

I'm glad I packed my camera bag with film and remembered to use it. Otherwise, I wouldn't know if the stories I'm telling were fact or fiction. According to the photos, I hugged a koala bear, thanks to Mrs. Freeman and her Wildworld. The picture prompts the viewer to ponder which was the most doped up: the bear full of eucalyptus leaves or me full of pain killers.

Time fogged by, and the day I left, Thursday, transmogrified into Wednesday across the International Date Line. I had two Wednesdays and two Thursdays in one week. Honestly. A nine day week. I hoped that idea never came to America. The school kids wouldn't like it.

By now, I didn't care if I was getting younger or older. All that mattered was making it through the 28-hour infinity of planes and airports between me and the one who gave me the kiss an eon ago. In the meantime, I wished the luggage dollies were beefy enough to carry me, too.

I know that I never, never should have gone. But through my smog of drugs, I gained some clear truths. And here they are:

Heartaches are written in the same key on every continent.

A Hurting Disciple

Faces need not be the same shape or the same color. Behind each one, pain is a common denominator. My young Thursday Island friend who played the guitar had less than a year to live with a kidney disease. Our pain brought us to a mutual understanding though our cultures were different. I hope that I was able to help her with her inner struggles. Her courage helped me. After our paths crossed, my own backpack seemed lighter.

Smiles come in different brands but are made with the same ingredients the world over. A smile transcends all language barriers and speaks one dialect. The tender smile says, "I love you." A sympathetic smile says, "I know what you're going through standing here in line at customs." The grateful smile says, "Thank you. You have made my job easier."

Thanks, Australia, land of the Never Never. You were good to this hurting disciple. I will never, never be the same after my tour to your land.

Stateside, my husband was standing at the airport, looking much like the revised version of a lost lad. I was still under the influence, but I did remember him. He was glad I had made it home safely to the land of my birth, the country I'll always love for its certain inherent rights. Among them: life, liberty and the pursuit of sanity.

A Blessed Disciple

As a child, I got five cents a week allowance. Minimum wage. That bought a round box of peanuts that might have a dime in it. It was worth a gamble. If you didn't get the dime, you could still eat the peanuts. And peanuts have lots of protein.

I could save my allowance from week to week, but I could not borrow in advance. It was a principle I learned early; to this day, I shy from borrowing anything.

By my high school years, my allowance had been increased to $1.00 a week. That was the ceiling. The maximum wage. I never got any more or any less throughout my school years, my working years and until I got married at age twenty-two.

When I returned from my honeymoon, there were two dollar bills on my dresser, one marked "His" and the other "Hers." The two dollar a week allowances found us wherever we roved for the next twenty years.

My mother took me aside one day before we set out to wend. She put two dollar bills (they were silver certificates then) into my hand. "Put these in your purse," she instructed. "If you break down on the road, use them to get help." They would buy a little gasoline, make a phone call or get a flat fixed in 1959. The

I'm Coming Apart, Lord!

thought that we might be stranded scourged her mind.

I had a wise pair of parents. Like a pen and pencil set, Dad was the pen and Mom the pencil. What Mom said could be erased with a little pleading, but Dad's words were indelible.

They could have done everything for us: handed us money, rented us an apartment, fueled our car. But we would never have grown. It must have been hard for Mom to stand and watch my struggle to iron that first white shirt for my husband, putting in more wrinkles than I took out. She could have taken the garment from my inexperienced hands and pressed it to perfection. She didn't. She let me sprinkle it with my tears of frustration and learn.

But Mom couldn't resist the gift of the two silver certificates. Her own peace of mind was folded up with them. From purse to purse the dollar bills rode, always with me, and not another soul knew that they were there.

For three years, we traveled without a travel trailer. That meant that everything we possessed must be compressed into one overwrought car. Carrying such a load was hard on a vehicle's internal organs, not to mention its spine. Over the half million miles, we had plenty of chances for breakdowns.

Fortunately, God had blessed me with a man gifted with ingenuity (engine-newity). He performed surgery on more motors than some doctors perform on patients. No contraption with bolts and nuts intimidated him since he kept a box of repair trivia between his ears. He could get more miles out of a car than General Motors put in it.

If he didn't have what it took to fix something, he would simply invent it. A lost cork while fishing? Substitute an empty sewing thread spool. If he lost the "skirt" off his lure, he could shred one of the children's balloons. No problem. Bait for his fishhooks might be a brand new menu for the fish.

A Blessed Disciple

So when the fanbelt broke while driving through a barren stretch of nothingness, the two silver certificates lay very still and worried. They didn't want to part with me; they had been with me so long they had become attached to me.

But zippo, my husband borrowed one of the legs of my nylon hose and tied it around the pulley for a belt, and we were on our way to the next town that sold Gates or Delco.

Then there was another close call when the radiator hose burst miles from civilization. The certificates huddled in fear again. But wasted fright it was. The engine-eous man took his pocket knife, cut out the damaged section of hose, located a piece of pipe and inserted it into the vacant spot, securing it with baling wire. It worked like a charm.

But, hark! With the radiator hose fixed, we needed liquid to refill the radiator. Where would we get it? There was no water for miles. He used our gallon jug of iced tea and got into the next town Sweet 'n' Low.

Once an alternator belt broke. He tied the alternator in place with a coat hanger. The hanger hung in until we reached a place to hang our hats. Another sigh of relief from the certificates and from me.

On one momentous trip, I couldn't tell which was the most worn, the left rear tire or my husband. A half block from the trailer park, the tire went flat. We hobbled on in.

It was always I who was "looking for a city" on the map as we drove along. I had no sense of direction, but I knew that up was north and down was south. What more was necessary? I never got us lost. Miles added to the chances for a catastrophe and to my admiration for my husband. It seemed that with each sacrifice my Abraham made, there was always a ram with his horns caught in the thicket. A ram that spared my two silver certificates.

I'm Coming Apart, Lord!

As we went "I think I can" over the Great Divide, the transmission had a heat stroke and expired. We coasted down the mountain, depending too heavily on the brakes. They got hot and bothered, which bothered me, too. By some unfathomable miracle, we crept into a trailer park in the town of our next employ. The transmission was gone. When daylight came, we looked around. Should we be surprised that there was a transmission shop across the street?

My silver certificates were still with me, getting more spoiled to their own bed every day. There were times I forgot about them as they slept.

Fourteen years after my mother gave me those two dollar bills, we moved into our permanent home. By now, America's currency had switched to Federal Reserve Notes. The Silver Certificates had been retired. (I've never trusted those notes like I trusted the certificates.)

"Please buy me a picture frame," I requested of my husband on one of his many trips to town as we settled into our new home.

"Why do you want a picture frame?"

"I need to frame these two bills." I showed him the bills and told him my long kept secret. "For victory. Because I never had to use them. God never once left us sitting beside the road!"

My husband thinks that the big victory was that a mall-loving woman like me could tote two dollar bills around for fourteen years without spending them and without telling.

I have those silver certificates yet. They wouldn't be worth anything to anybody else, but to me they are worth all the gold in Fort Knox. They remind me of God's golden promises to take care of His children.

I hope to keep them all the way to the New Jerusalem.

A Mellowing Disciple

We're older now, and though we're not quite to the twilight zone, we haven't the wattage we had all those light years ago. Granted, some days we don't know whatt is watt, and the rocking chair looks better and better. But show me to an outlet, and watch me plug right in.

"I'll try to remember our names if you'll remember where we are going," I tell my sweet thing. I'm glad our church is patient with dim-witted patients.

Recently, we celebrated our tenth adversary with the Morris Untied Pentecostal Church. I wrote them a book, a hysterical work that they could keep for their prosperity. Like measles, it is too catchy not to spread around (according to our saints), so to humor them, I include this chapter, sharing a few punch lines just for fun. (You who are smart enough to shun puns may skip this chapter and go directly to page 138.)

The church was split three ways when we got here. There were those who were Hurt (that was their name) or had been. Then there were the Vaughans with A Vaughan representative. (Avon, get it?) All the rest were nice, mixed-up people like the Caseys and Stacys and other names that didn't rhyme.

I'm Coming Apart, Lord!

We moved into the parsonage, hung pictures of our kinfolks on the walls and gathered some furniture that had been through a tornado furnished by two sisters. A kind man in the church threw a newspaper every morning so we would know if the world blew to smithereens. It never did.

The church made pizzas for a living; some were Supreme. They fished for orders from the Bank, which was across the street. They sold other places for reasonable prices. Individuals sometimes bought, but they were uncooked.

We made the pizzas with an ironing board, and the cheese had scales. We workers ate some of the profit at the end. We made money, which I think is against the law, but we were trying to get out of debt fast.

The Sunday School supervisor wanted more of everybody. His wife was a teller (at the Bank), and his son had two horns. He grew up to be a preacher; people with horns usually do. He was kin to us, once removed.

The church secretary was a good woman, too. She kept up with the money, which is more than most women can do. Her husband fixes cars and fries turkeys of any model and make during the holidays.

The head deacon had a pontoon boat; it was his Hobby Lobby. He lived in the same house for so long that his married daughter sometimes rearranged things while they were gone to the lake changing the carpet. The deacon used to be tired; now he is retired. That's like being tired all over again only worse.

My brother, whose name is Berry, transplanted here. He was ripe for a change. He set up a shop and painted cars. He did really good work. He painted them so they would never run as runs are bad for paint. A young bachelor in the church picked the elder-Berry girl. His name is Foster, and they had two Foster children.

A Mellowing Disciple

My brother also writes the church paper on weak ends. He stays up half the night Saturdays trying to think how to wish people a happy birthday so they'll be cheerful about getting older. Then he's droopy on Sunday mornings. If we want something told, he'll tell it a week ahead even if it hasn't happened yet but might.

One of our lay ministers sings in Spanish, but the musicians play in English. It takes a lot of consecration to follow it with your mind. He and his wife have a big trailer and a little trailer so they can pull it with their car behind. His wife knits sweaters and reads the Bible through with her hip replacement every year. They take in homeless children and keep the kids' pictures in their pocketbooks with their AARP cards ever after.

Everybody in our church is tangled up worse than a ball of yarn that a cat snarled. Everybody is relative to someone else. We're kin to the Berries who are kin to the Fosters who are kin to the Stacys and the Dennises and the Joneses. The Whitakers are kin to the Corns and the Staffords and the Norwoods and the Hamptons and the Hurts. A new convert came along with blonde hair and married a Jordan who was kin to the Berrys who were kin to the Fosters who were kin to the Stacys–and us? Anyhow, the Jordan couple had twins, so now they won't have to cross Jordan alone.

With all the intertwining, we've found it's best not to badmouth anybody. You might be depreciating your own grandpa. And you can't claim that depreciation off your income tax.

The culprit that really tied everything in double-bow knots was our own middle child. She went to two Bridal Schools only to come home and marry a Hurt. Now everybody is connected, and our grandbabies are in the potpourri somewhere. Our daughter's husband is a fireman. He is off for forty-eight hours of the time.

The cleaning lady watches the supply closet and reminds the pastor when the church needs more Joy. He puts it on the list with

I'm Coming Apart, Lord!

bleach and paper towels and trash bags, and we get it at Sam's.

Aunt Lucy is special. She has been in the flock longer than anyone else for 75 years. She plays the piano once a year for the penny march on Old Fashioned Sunday. She'll be playing When the Saints Go Marching In.

Her sister, Ollie, is the next oldest. She has made blackberry cobblers for church dinners for 62 years. When she walks up and down the aisle praising God with her bum knees, the whole church goes bonkers. They've both together been coming to church for 137 years.

Our organist is Fran. She should have a Fran-chise because she sits on the organ bench and plays with her feet. Also, she's a music teacher who gives concerts twice a year with her high blood pressure. It is chronically a success. Her husband whistles. I tell about him when I go speak, and now he's famous. He can stop leaks and unstop things. He makes cinnamon rolls a hundred times better than Daylight Donuts.

Our piano player can play well with her ear. Her husband is a trustee. That's someone you can trust to a tee. They have a cellar that's free to everybody with no rent in case of a storm, but it doesn't have anything in it that shouldn't be there. We checked it out.

We've had some strange romances. One gentleman fell in love with a set of long fingernails, and they snagged him. That was his own admission. Then a girl named Karen lost her heart to a Hart. And Scott Hart gave her his Hart. Wasn't that a sweet-Hart? She gets a break where she works, and we wonder if that would be called a Hart-break. Scott brings a glass of water to the pastor every service. That helps whet the sermons.

We had a wonderful chorale that made a singing tape. We thought they were better than Brooklyn Tab. (That's a fancy choir

A Mellowing Disciple

from New York or somewhere.) The chorale practiced until their tonsils were sore; then they traveled, and that helped. We all gave money and unnecessary advice.

Over the years our youth did walk-a-things, car sloshes, garbage sales, and, oh, yes, they made sticky sucker bears from syrup. What they couldn't sell, they ate. It was a case of lambs eating bears. It was a woolly project. And once they sold fruitcakes. Our daughter used ten dollars worth of gasoline to sell two dollars worth of cakes. The car gave her E for effort.

They did quizzing, too. They slapped buzzers and won trophies. Once they went all the way to Louisiana and had to stay all night in a tournament because it was so far. We had an invitational at our church, which was a lot different from an altar call. We served cold hot dogs.

We have a college near us, and a handsome guy came to our church getting his classes. He was on loan to us from another church, but the interest was very high. Almost 100 percent. The girls paid it.

We have a clown in the church. She makes balloons into baboons. Once she went to Tennessee with me and impersonalized Elvis. She brought the house down. She had a job selling Dooney & Burke purses, but the bottom kind of dropped out. Nobody likes all work and no pay.

The milkman's wife used to be in our church. Then she moved away. We liked it when she was here and brought her other half to service because that way we had half-and-half.

The children liked their program called Kids' Stuff. It was a workshop to teach them and to eat once a month. They learned active songs and other crafty things. They collected Kans for Kids and bottle lids. All of us tried to save them. One older boy brought his little brother who always wore a hood in cold weather. That's

I'm Coming Apart, Lord!

real brotherhood.

We have a photographer in our church, and that doesn't pose a problem. She made a smooth finish of her education with no negatives. (Oh, cum laude.) She's good at mug shots, and she'll practice on anybody who will sit still and some who won't. She took a picture of us, but we aren't very photogenius.

A bad wreck that wrecked my husband's legs–he was in the right lane–caused a trial at the courthouse. One of our sheep was a dejected juror. She almost gave the opposing lawyer's cardiac a rest when she said something nice and bias about her pastor which the whole courtroom heard. The lawyer about ruptured a disk trying to get her shut down.

We have a recording secretary, but her records don't sing or play music. They help with your Form 1040 or whatever shape you happen to be in with the IRS. Her husband is an usher who shows people to their seats when they are lost. He also passes out. Bulletins.

A lady had a secret burden for secret pals. Of course, everybody knows which secret pal everybody else has but isn't supposed to know. They pretend they don't know and act surprised when it's time to tell. We all like to get teapots and macrame and senseless candles. (Misprint. That should have been scented candles.) Sometimes secret pals give other secret pals something they got from their secret pal, and it gets to be a scream.

Finally, the sheep got their Shepherd a car phone so they could keep up with him remotely. It didn't work because he always forgot to turn it on. Except one time it didn't get turned off, and the phone bill was you don't want to know what. But the cellular company was kind enough to knock it off since it was an honest-to-badness mistake.

Somewhere in these ten years, I started going astray. From

A Mellowing Disciple

see to shining see. When I have to make a long car trip (I like long cars), I take someone with me as my auto pilot. Sometimes it is my daughter, sometimes my sister-in-law or a friend. Anybody who is flexible. Sometimes we get locked out on balconies or take wrong highways or lose something important or run out of gas.

Then I started writing books. And more books. And books and books and books until the closets got cluttered and my family muttered. My daughter wanted to fire me and get another mother, but my husband vetoed that. He thought a new spouse might not have as much spice.

But now it is time to bring our train of thought to the terminal. I know it was a bad voyage, but there are no refunds. Sorry.

A Growing Disciple

Writing a book isn't instant pudding. It is slaving over a raw manuscript–mixing and stirring and kneading–until it takes on the right viscosity for a happy outcome. It can't be too tough, too thin, too flat, too dense or too flaky.

Words can be rascals. They fuss and fight, kiss and make up and then scrap some more. They keep you up at night, hide under objects and follow you to choir practice on Sunday afternoon.

Whatever its beginning, a book must have a proper ending. A colorful caboose. A lantern swinging brakeman. And tail lights that melt into the distance, leaving lingering memories.

Remember when you were a child, driven about by every tune of the ice cream man? Remember the birthday celebrations? Blowing out the candles? Pinning the tail on the donkey? And remember when you were open game for everyone's paddle? It was one lick per year. And then one to grow on. That extra swat carried more oomph, had more clobber power. It was a special wallop, outsmarting all the others.

As I close the chapters of *I'm Coming Apart Lord. Does That Mean I'm A Disciple?*, I want to leave you one to grow on.

To this end, I asked my husband's permission to use a

I'm Coming Apart, Lord!

beautiful piece of free verse that he authored. I can think of no more perfect conclusion.

THE WEAVER

Upon the loom of my heart
    I wove the threads of my thought
Until the tapestry made
    Became a picture of me.
My borders scarce defined, in shadowed grays,
In childlike patterns of uncertain ways,
    Left unfinished for lack of
        planned things to be.
The scheme of things came softly and shyly
To be interrupted by splashes of bold skeins
    Began suddenly to only end
    Abruptly with no place to go.
As years came into the web and woof,
    So came the consistent patterns of habit
    Formed and seldom changed.
Now you have a character born,
    An image seen.
'Twill be one of darker shades
With only an occasional blend
    Of color bright and clean.
Oh! If it could be woven again,
    By hands so right and true

A Growing Disciple

Might this one woeful rug
    Could a better one be and do.
Could the Master of life's craft
    Make another one in time so short?
Impossible I say,
    Far too much time was spent
    And that many years will not again be lent.
Ah, but says He, I will take this one
    And let's begin another,
Tho' it will not be as long and wide.
Because its quality and design will be so perfect
    Its worth shall be many times more
Than scores of those . . . of the kind you once wore.

God Bless You. L.M.